beyond the
blues

a workbook to help teens
overcome **depression**

LISA M. SCHAB, LCSW

Instant Help Books
A Division of New Harbinger Publications, Inc.

Distributed in Canada by Raincoast Books

Copyright © 2008 by Lisa M. Schab
Instant Help Books
A Division of New Harbinger Publications, Inc.
5674 Shattuck Avenue
Oakland, CA 94609
www.newharbinger.com

Cover design by Amy Shoup
Illustrations by Julie Olson

Library of Congress Cataloging-in-Publication Data

Schab, Lisa M.
  Beyond the blues : a workbook to help teens overcome depression / Lisa M. Schab.
    p. cm.
  ISBN-13: 978-1-57224-611-9 (pbk. : alk. paper)
  ISBN-10: 1-57224-611-1 (pbk. : alk. paper) 1. Depression in adolescence--Popular works. 2. Teenagers--Mental health--Popular works. I. Title.
  RJ506.D4S33 2008
  618.92'85270078--dc22

                                             2008003636

FSC
Mixed Sources
Product group from well-managed forests and other controlled sources
Cert no. SW-COC-002283
www.fsc.org
© 1996 Forest Stewardship Council

11   10   09

10   9   8   7   6   5   4

contents

introduction

Dear Reader,

Many people experience depression at one time or another in their lives, but during the adolescent years, the vast number of physical, emotional, and mental changes that occur make teens even more susceptible to feelings of confusion or sadness. However your depression originates, you will need to learn to handle it so that you can go about your daily life and be happy.

Whether your feelings of depression are mild or intense, long term or temporary, inherited or situational, you can be helped by working through the exercises in this book. They are not meant to replace other treatments, but to supplement them, so you may also talk to a counselor or take medication for depression. Remember that working on managing depression is similar to taking a class or learning anything new: the more you put into it, the more you will get out of it. If you skim through this book, you can learn a little; if you really explore and work through the exercises, you can make your life better.

Since everyone is different and heals in slightly different ways, a wide variety of exercises have been presented. It is your job to investigate them all and find the ones that are right for you. Each time you try an exercise, think of it as an experiment. Your goal is to learn something about yourself. If one exercise doesn't work well for you, it doesn't mean you have failed. It means you have learned that the exercise isn't the right one for you at this moment. Keep going until you find something that does work. You may have to give some activities a second or third try until you feel comfortable, and that's normal.

It is important to remember that if your feelings of depression do not go away, if they get worse, or if they begin to frighten you, you must tell someone who can help to keep you safe. Several of the exercises at the end of the book talk about this. Be sure to share them with an adult who can help you.

Know that as you work through this book, you are doing something good for yourself. You are learning to cope with your feelings and take care of yourself in a healthy way.

You can learn to manage depression just like you learned to tie your shoes or read and write. Just give it a chance and be patient with yourself. You deserve to feel good, and you will if you keep working at it!

Lisa M. Schab, LCSW

defining depression 1

you need to know
Depression is a disturbance in someone's mood. It usually involves a feeling of sadness, a lack of physical and emotional energy, and a loss of interest in things that used to bring pleasure. Depression is one of the most common emotional problems and also one of the most treatable.

Everyone has days when they feel more happy or more sad. You may feel great when your team wins the championship, when you get a good grade on a test, or when you are having fun at a party. You may feel really down when you have an argument with your best friend, when your parents won't let you go to a concert, or when you don't get a part in the school play. Normal sadness passes in a reasonable amount of time, and soon you are feeling better again.

Depression lasts longer and feels deeper than normal sadness. It may cause you to feel very bad about yourself or hopeless about your future. It may affect your thoughts, your behavior, your appetite, or your ability to sleep. Depression may cause you to see reality in a distorted way, as if everything is negative and difficult, and problems may appear to be bigger than you can bear.

People who feel depressed often feel very tired physically and emotionally. They may stop spending time with friends or doing other things that used to give them pleasure, because they just don't feel up to it. They may also start to complain of physical problems, such as headaches and stomachaches. At its worst, depression can make people feel as if they don't want to be alive.

The more you understand about depression and the more you learn about how to combat it, the easier it will be to either manage these feelings or eliminate them altogether. The exercises in this book can help you to do this.

directions

In the space below, use line, color, texture, or form to show what your feelings of depression would look like if you could see them.

more to do

Look back at your picture and describe what you have drawn. Tell why you used the lines, colors, textures, and forms that you did.

_____

_____

Describe how you feel when you look at your picture.

_____

_____

Describe what you have already tried to do to relieve feelings of depression. Tell how well each of these things worked for you.

_____

_____

Think about the fact that you can learn new ways to cope with and combat depression. Tell what you believe or how you feel about this fact.

_____

_____

Write a statement that describes your commitment to learning how to deal with depression. Make a conscious decision to keep that commitment.

_____

_____

2 symptoms of depression

you need to know

There are many symptoms of depression. Some of them are very clear, and some may seem confusing. Each person's symptoms and experience of depression may be a little different from everyone else's. Learning to recognize your own symptoms can help you to both prevent and manage depression.

Blake has been getting into trouble lately. He can't seem to control his temper at school or at home, and he is snapping at everyone, including his teachers. He has been cutting classes because it just seems easier than having to face people. Instead of going to class, he walks to the convenience store and smokes cigarettes in the parking lot. He thinks about running away and wonders where he could go.

Sabrina's friends are worried about her. She hasn't been returning their calls and seems distracted and spacey at school. When she comes out of the bathroom her eyes sometimes look red, as if she's been crying. She often goes home right after school instead of hanging out to shoot baskets like she used to. When her friends ask what is wrong, Sabrina just shrugs and says, "I don't know."

Maddie has been having trouble sleeping. She lies in bed and stares at the ceiling for hours, thinking about all the things she did wrong that day. Her grades have been slipping because she keeps forgetting her homework. She always seems tired and has no interest in eating. She feels bad about herself and wishes she could be "normal" and "cool" like her friends.

All three of these teens are feeling depressed, but they are experiencing different symptoms.

directions

All of the symptoms below may be expressions of depression. Circle any that you have experienced.

trouble sleeping	unhappiness	significant weight change
reckless behavior	drug abuse	withdrawal from friends
feeling helpless	constant boredom	skipping classes often
fear of death	increased irritability	no interest in activities
alcohol abuse	feeling worthless	increase in sex drive
trouble focusing	achy body parts	constant desire to be alone
increased anger	difficulty making decisions	overly negative attitude
frequent crying	strong feelings of guilt	feeling like a failure
self-injury	suicidal thoughts	disappointment in self
physical aggression	forgetfulness	missing appointments
decrease in sex drive	increased family conflicts	withdrawal into self
no interest in hygiene	constant restlessness	thoughts of running away

Describe anything else you have experienced that you think may be a symptom of depression.

_____

_____

_____

_____

more to do

It is normal for anyone to experience symptoms of depression at one time or another. Symptoms may come and go over the course of days, weeks, or months. Symptoms become a problem if they cause a long-term or severe disturbance in your life. Examples would be a feeling of sadness that causes you to quit the swim team, angry outbursts that drive away your friends, or feelings of such discomfort that you make cuts on your skin to try to relieve the emotional pain.

Look back over the symptoms that you circled. List the ones that come and go but don't cause much disruption in your life.

_____

_____

_____

_____

Now list the symptoms that cause a long-term or severe disturbance in your life. Next to each one, tell how long it lasts and how it disrupts your life.

_____

_____

_____

_____

_____

_____

Share the information about your severe symptoms with an adult, such as a parent, teacher, doctor, nurse, or counselor.

causes of depression   3

you need to know

Just as depression has different symptoms in different people, it also has a number of different causes. The most common causes of depression include experiencing difficult life events, living in a negative family or social environment, personality type, physical illness, medications, biochemical factors, genetics, and alcohol or drug abuse. Usually more than one factor contributes to a person's depression.

An environment is a person's surroundings. Negative family or social environments might include those in which there is poverty, hunger, emotional abuse, physical abuse, crime, high degrees of conflict, poor communication, violence, instability, unsanitary conditions, or neglect of children.

Personality type affects people's perspective on life, other people, and themselves. Personalities that are more vulnerable to depression are those with an unrealistic or negative focus, such as perfectionistic, highly self-critical, overly passive or dependent, or highly anxious.

Physical illness that is very severe or long-term can drain people of their physical and emotional energy. Some illnesses may handicap people either temporarily or permanently, limiting them or changing their ability to function as they once used to. Other illnesses can affect certain glands in the body and create a depressed mood.

While the purpose of medication is to help people feel better, some types can affect their brain chemistry in a way that causes them to feel depressed.

Although we are not generally aware of it, we each have a certain number, type, and balance of chemicals flowing through our brains at all times. If there is a shortage of these chemicals, or if they get out of balance, depression can occur. Chemicals may shift in balance because of hormonal changes (such as those during puberty and adolescence), nutrition, exercise, and seasonal changes.

We inherit both physical and emotional characteristics from our parents, grandparents, great-grandparents, and beyond. The traits we get from our ancestors are said to be genetic. Vulnerability to depression tends to run in families.

Alcohol and street drugs can cause chemical changes in the brain that affect people's moods. While people often use alcohol and drugs to try to make themselves feel good, the opposite occurs physiologically, and they become more depressed instead.

directions

Draw or paste a picture of yourself in the center box below. In each of the labeled boxes, list or describe any factors in that category that are present or have been present in your life. If you have not been affected by a category, leave it blank. Then draw a line from each box you have written in to your picture in the middle.

Life Events

Social Environment

Personality Type

Physical Illness

Medications

Biochemical Factors

Genetics

Family Environment

Alcohol or Drug Abuse

more to do

Look at your completed picture and labeled boxes. What do they tell you about yourself?

_____

_____

List the categories that have affected you in order of their importance. For example, if you think that genetics has affected you the most, list it first. If you think that personality type has affected you the least, list it last.

1. _____   6. _____

2. _____   7. _____

3. _____   8. _____

4. _____   9. _____

5. _____

Which categories do you feel you have some control over? Which do you feel you have no control over?

_____

_____

Your completed picture can tell you some of the causes of your depression. Realizing what might have contributed to your feeling depressed, describe any ideas you have for overcoming your depression.

_____

_____

_____

you need to know

Many people enjoy light, sunny days more than dark, cloudy days. But some people are so sensitive to the amount of light they receive that it can affect their moods to a stronger degree. People who become very depressed during the darker winter months may suffer from a condition called seasonal affective disorder (SAD). A milder form of this condition is called the "winter blues."

Exposure to light and dark has an effect on our bodies. Melatonin, a chemical related to sleep, is produced more when it is dark. Serotonin, a chemical related to feeling good, is produced more when it is light. During the winter months when there is less sunlight, some people's bodies produce such a great amount of melatonin and such a small amount of serotonin that they can start to feel depressed. Symptoms of seasonal disorders can include depression, irritability, lack of energy, increased need for sleep, craving for sweets, overeating, weight gain, difficulty concentrating, and decrease of interest in social activities. These symptoms may begin as early as autumn, reach their peak in January and February, and decrease again in spring.

If you experience symptoms of SAD or winter blues, you can help yourself in these ways:

- Educate yourself, your friends, and your family about these conditions.

- Try phototherapy, or "light therapy." Exposure to special bright-light boxes can reduce depressive symptoms in some people.

- Use higher-wattage bulbs or full-spectrum bulbs.

- Increase your exposure to outdoor light by spending more time outdoors, clearing windows and doors of heavy draperies, rearranging work spaces so that you spend more time near a window, or sitting next to windows in public places.

- Exercise on a regular basis, outdoors if possible, or indoors near a window.

- Ask for help with schoolwork if you have a hard time concentrating.

- Try to eat nutritiously to keep your energy level up and your health stable.

- Try to keep a stable sleep routine and remain awake during as many daylight hours as possible.

- Make it easier for yourself to awaken by putting your bedroom lights on a timer that turns on thirty minutes before you get up.

- Take a vacation to a warmer, sunnier climate, if possible.

- Talk to a counselor about your feelings and learn healthy ways to cope.

directions

Think about whether you are strongly affected by the change in sunlight throughout the year. For each category below, color the appropriate number of suns to show how much you are affected during the winter months.

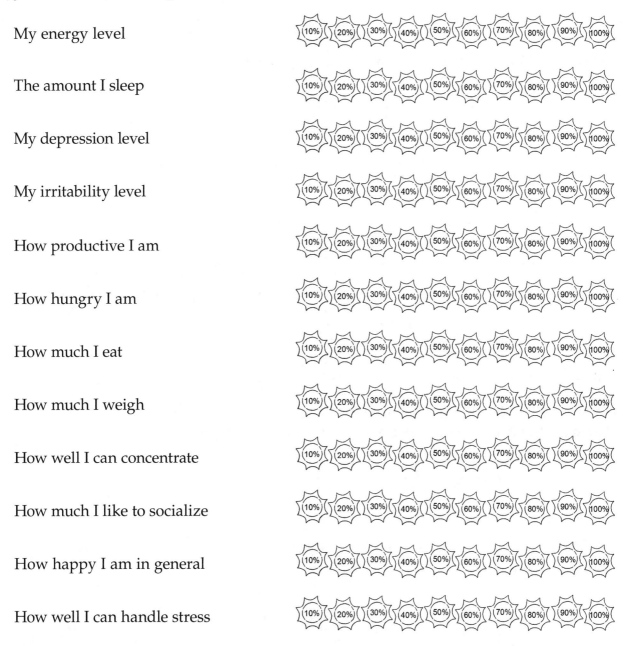

My energy level

The amount I sleep

My depression level

My irritability level

How productive I am

How hungry I am

How much I eat

How much I weigh

How well I can concentrate

How much I like to socialize

How happy I am in general

How well I can handle stress

After you have rated yourself, ask someone who knows you well and spends a lot of time with you (maybe someone who lives in your house) to rate you.

more to do

Look back at your ratings and list the categories you have rated 50 percent or lower.

_____

_____

List the categories you have rated more than 50 percent.

_____

_____

Describe how your two lists compare.

_____

_____

Describe how your ratings compare to the ratings of the other person who rated you.

_____

_____

Based on all of these ratings, make an overall observation about how closely your characteristics resemble those of someone with seasonal depression.

_____

_____

Tell which of the coping ideas you think would best help you manage your seasonal feelings of depression.

_____

_____

the negative effects of alcohol and street drugs 5

you need to know

Some people want so much to escape from their feelings of depression that they use mood-altering substances, such as alcohol or street drugs, to try to feel better quickly. Unfortunately, because of the way they affect the brain, these substances only end up making the depression worse. Instead of helping the problem, alcohol and street drugs only make the problem bigger.

When people try to self-medicate by using alcohol or street drugs to make them feel better, they may feel good at first, but eventually they end up feeling worse than when they started. This is because with repeated use these substances damage brain receptors and brain messengers, called neurotransmitters.

Neurotransmitters are chemicals that help in transmitting messages between nerve cells in the brain. Certain neurotransmitters regulate people's moods. Alcohol and street drugs can damage these neurotransmitters, making users feel depressed even if they weren't to begin with.

Alcohol and drug use can also contribute to depressing situations and behaviors, such as decreased school performance, problems with family and social relationships, poor concentration, and low energy levels. Being arrested for illegal use of alcohol or drugs creates a life event that also contributes to depression. Alcohol and street drugs are "quick fixes" that end up not being able to fix anything at all.

directions

Most quick fixes in life do not provide effective solutions to problems. Next to each set of pictures below, tell why the quick answer may work temporarily but will not actually fix the problem in the long run.

_____

_____

_____

_____

_____

_____

_____

_____

_____

_____

more to do

Describe a situation where you tried to use a quick fix to solve a problem. Tell if the quick fix solved the problem permanently.

_____

_____

What would actually have been required to solve the problem permanently?

_____

_____

Describe a situation where a family member or friend tried to use a quick fix to solve a problem. Tell if the quick fix solved the problem permanently.

_____

_____

What would actually have been required to solve the problem permanently?

_____

_____

Why do you think people try to use quick fixes if they know that these won't really solve problems permanently?

_____

_____

How can using alcohol or street drugs make you end up feeling even more depressed?

_____

_____

choosing positive thoughts

you need to know

The way people think directly affects their moods. One way to combat feelings of depression is by practicing positive thinking instead of negative thinking.

Cameron had just gotten home from the jazz band competition, and he was feeling depressed. His mom noticed that he looked sad and asked him how the competition had gone. Cameron said that something upsetting had happened: he had received an award for his performance on the saxophone.

His mom asked why that made him feel upset. Cameron said that he didn't think he deserved the award, and now he would feel pressured to live up to it. Then he said that the band director was giving a party for him. Cameron's mom said that sounded like fun, but Cameron told her that the party would be at a restaurant that held bad memories for him. It was the last place he had been with his girlfriend before she broke up with him.

When Cameron's mom suggested he try to go anyway, Cameron told her there was more. The band director was presenting him with a gift certificate to a music store at a nearby mall. Cameron's mom thought that was an appropriate and generous gift, but Cameron reminded her that he hated going to the mall because it was so noisy and crowded.

Cameron's mom finally told him, "Situations are not negative or positive within themselves. It is the thoughts we choose to think about them that make us feel happy or depressed. You are feeling depressed because you are choosing to think negative thoughts about everything. If you choose to think positive thoughts, you will feel much better." They talked about it together, and Cameron decided on these changes:

Negative Thoughts	Positive Thoughts
"I don't deserve the award; now I'll feel pressured to live up to it."	"I trust the band director's judgment. If he chose me for the award, I must deserve it."
"I will feel terrible going to that restaurant because of the bad memories."	"I can't avoid that restaurant forever. This is a good chance to create new, positive memories there."
"I'll have to go to the mall, which I don't like, to redeem that gift certificate."	"Now I can get the CD I've been wanting. I don't have to hang out in the mall. I'll just go into the music store and then leave."

When Cameron changed his thoughts from negative to positive, his mood changed, too.

directions

Think of a situation in your life that you feel depressed about. Below the picture on the left, write the negative thoughts you are thinking that make you feel depressed. Draw your face to show how you feel. Below the picture on the right, write positive thoughts you could think to feel good instead of depressed. Draw your face to show how these positive thoughts would make you feel.

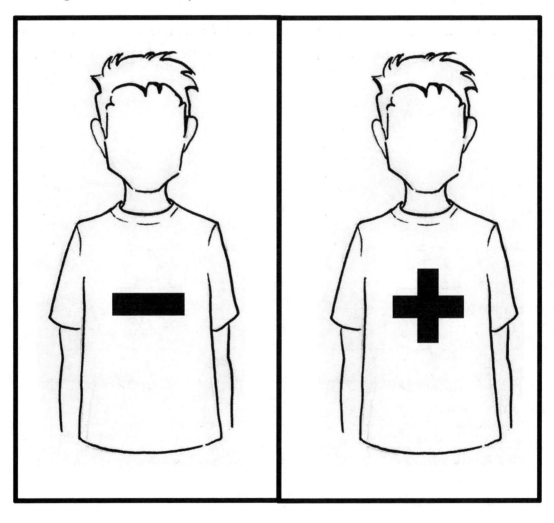

more to do

Changing our thoughts to change our feelings is a simple idea, but it is not always easy to do. Some life situations are very difficult, and it is hard to think about them in a positive way. Tell how hard or easy it would be to change your thoughts about the situation you described above.

_____

_____

For each situation below, write a positive statement that could make someone feel happy about it, and then write a negative statement that could make someone feel depressed about it.

Being youngest in the family

_____

_____

Being very tall

_____

_____

Going to a party

_____

_____

Getting a new puppy

_____

_____

Being elected class president

_____

_____

School closing because of bad weather

_____

_____

Being the first one to give your oral report

_____

_____

Taking a test

_____

_____

Being an only child

_____

_____

Being last in line for the roller coaster

_____

_____

Summer ending

_____

_____

Moving to a new town

_____

_____

Think of something that happened to you in the last week that you felt happy about. Write the positive thoughts you told yourself that made you feel happy about this.

_____

_____

_____

Now write two or more negative thoughts that could have made you feel depressed about this.

_____

_____

_____

_____

_____

Think of something that happened to you in the last week that you felt depressed about. Write the negative thoughts you told yourself that made you feel depressed about this.

_____

_____

_____

Now write two or more positive thoughts that could have made you feel happy about this.

_____

_____

_____

_____

Remember that you are the only one that can choose your thoughts!

the power of perspective 7

you need to know

Some people act as if every occurrence in their life is crucial to their happiness. With that perspective, they may easily feel depressed when something turns out different from the way they had hoped. Putting life circumstances into a broader perspective can help you to withstand disappointments and maintain a positive mood.

Desiree started out the day feeling happy, but when she got on the school bus, there were no seats left next to her friends. She had to sit in the back with someone she didn't know. For the entire twenty-minute ride, she kept looking at her friends, who were laughing at the front of the bus, and thinking about how disappointed she was that she couldn't be with them. She thought about the unfairness of it all and wondered why she couldn't have had better luck. She thought about how much fun she could be having, rather than wasting the whole bus ride doing nothing and being bored. When the bus finally arrived at school, Desiree's mood was low, and she avoided her friends when they tried to talk to her. She was focused on her thoughts of how everything bad always seemed to happen to her.

Desiree's mood got lower and lower because she viewed one occurrence—where she sat on the bus—as crucial to her happiness. In her mind, she saw this minor incident as a very big setback. It was as if she put this one small occurrence under a microscope and magnified it a hundred times.

If Desiree's perspective were different, she could have told herself: "I wish there were seats left next to my friends. Oh well, it's only a twenty-minute ride; I'll talk with them when we get to school." She could have daydreamed or looked out the window during the bus ride and then caught up with her friends when they got off the bus. If she had taken the perspective that the bus ride was a minor incident, her mood could have been happy instead of depressed.

directions

The people in the pictures that follow are each experiencing situations that are not turning out the way they had hoped. Put each situation "under a microscope" and describe it as if it were a very big setback. Tell how each of these people would feel if they chose this perspective. On the second group of lines, describe the situation from the perspective of its being a minor occurrence. Tell how the people would feel if they chose this perspective.

more to do

Describe three things that happened to you over the past week that didn't turn out the way you had hoped, and the perspective you took on each. Tell how this perspective made you feel.

1. _____

2. _____

3. _____

If any of your perspectives made you feel depressed, write a different perspective you could have taken that would have made you feel happier.

1. _____

2. _____

3. _____

Tell which you think is easier to choose: a perspective that makes you feel depressed or one that makes you feel happy.

_____

Tell why you think it might be hard for some people to change their perspective.

_____

_____

Tell why you think it could be worthwhile to change your perspective, even if it takes work.

_____

_____

Tell how you think your own choice of perspective does or does not contribute to your feelings of depression.

_____

_____

learning to let go

Marc and Kevin were twins. They were alike in many ways; their hair color and the turn of their smiles were identical. They both liked the same kind of music and downhill skiing. One way they were very different, however, was in how they handled difficulties. When Marc was upset, he would sit in his room stewing for hours. He often felt depressed. When something was bothering Kevin, he would share his feelings with someone, do what he could to fix it, and then try to let it go, knowing that dwelling on it would only make him feel worse. As a result, Kevin felt depressed far less often than Marc.

When the boys found out their family was moving, they were both upset. They didn't want to leave their familiar surroundings. They talked about it, agreeing that they wished they could stay in their current home. Then, Marc went up to his room and started thinking about how his life would be changing. He thought about the good friends he would have to leave. He thought about going to a completely new place where he wouldn't know anybody, and he wondered what kids would think about him. He thought about how awful it would be if he couldn't make any new friends. He thought about leaving the baseball team and the ballpark where he played every Saturday. Marc continued to dwell on all the hard parts of the upcoming move, and he finally fell asleep feeling depressed. The next morning he didn't feel like getting up, much less going to school.

Kevin was also upset about the move. He thought about what a big change it would make in his life, and how he would miss his friends. He even went to his best friend's house and told him about it. They decided they would e-mail each other every day and try to spend the next school vacation together. After talking about it a while, Kevin said, "Well, there's nothing I can do to change it, and we still have plans for the movies. Let's go." The boys went to see a great movie, and Kevin came home feeling good. Whenever he found himself feeling sad or concerned about the move, he would talk with his family or friends about it and then turn his mind to something else.

Facing the same situation, Marc felt depressed because he held on to the negative thoughts. Kevin felt happier because he talked about these thoughts and then he let them go.

directions

Kevin was able to let go of his negative thoughts by talking with someone about them and then turning his mind to something else. There are other ways to help yourself let go as well.

Exercise 1

On a separate sheet of paper, describe a problem that has been making you feel depressed lately. Write about it in as much detail as you can. Choose one of the methods below to physically let go of what you have written, and then do it. As you destroy your problem, tell yourself, "I am letting go of this. I will not let it depress me anymore."

- Rip up your paper into tiny pieces and throw it into the garbage.

- Put your paper through a shredder.

- Read what you have written to someone else and then give that person the paper and ask him or her to rip it up in front of you.

- With permission and in the presence of an adult, burn your paper in a fireplace.

- With permission and in the presence of an adult, poke a long stick through your paper and burn it over a grill.

- Write your problem on bathroom tissue instead of regular paper and flush it down the toilet.

Exercise 2

Sit quietly and comfortably where you will not be disturbed. Close your eyes and picture yourself in vivid detail doing one of the following:

- You wrap your problem in a box and seal it very securely with strong tape and rope. Then you attach the box to a very powerful rocket. You take the rocket to an outdoor area where there are no houses, trees, or other obstructions. You light the rocket and stand back. You watch as the rocket blasts off into the sky with great speed and force. You watch it carry your problem quickly and powerfully away from you. You watch until it is completely out of sight, far off beyond the pull of Earth's gravity, continuing to travel farther into space. As you watch it go, you say to yourself, "I am letting go of this. I will not let it depress me anymore."

- You wrap your problem in a box and seal it very securely with strong tape and rope. Then you travel to a place far from where you live. You come to the edge of an ocean. If the climate is warm, you set the box onto a very fragile raft. If the climate is cold, you set the box onto a very fragile ice floe. You push the raft or the ice floe out into the sea, where the current catches it and carries it farther and farther away from you. You watch it until it is completely out of sight. As you watch it go, you say to yourself, "I am letting go of this. I will not let it depress me anymore."

You may repeat either of these exercises as many times as you like, experimenting with different methods.

more to do

Describe what it was like to complete Exercise 1. Tell how it felt to watch the paper that described your problem be destroyed.

_____

_____

_____

_____

Describe what it was like to complete Exercise 2. Tell how it felt to watch the box holding your problem disappear in the distance.

_____

_____

_____

_____

Which, if either, exercise helped you feel that you had let go of your problem? Tell why.

_____

_____

_____

_____

If neither of these exercises was helpful to you the first time, try doing them using a different method from the list. Then, think up your own safe way to destroy your paper or another visualization that is effective for you. Describe your idea here.

_____

_____

_____

_____

9 the gift of the moment

you need to know

Some people have a habit of frequently looking into the future with a negative focus. They spend a lot of time predicting negative outcomes, missing the positive things that are happening to them in the present moment. This causes them to feel depressed. Keeping your mental focus on the positive qualities of the present can help you to combat depressive feelings.

Elana worked hard in school and got good grades. She had friends and a family that loved her, and she was healthy. But Elana felt more and more depressed every day. She didn't seem to get much pleasure from anything she did, and she was spending more time at home alone with her computer than out with her friends. Elana's mother was worried and took her to the doctor for a checkup.

The doctor could find nothing physically wrong with Elana, so she asked how her life was going. Elana said that she felt like everything she did was useless. She spent most of her time working hard in school to get good grades so she could get into a good college someday. She tried to get into clubs that would look good on a college application. She figured she would have to work hard in college and be involved in the right organizations there, too, so she could get a good job when she graduated. Then she figured she would have to work hard at her future job in order to pay all of her bills and save enough money to retire on. And then she figured that after all that hard work, she would probably have a heart attack and die. What was the point of doing anything at all?

The doctor said that Elana's thinking was so negatively focused on the future that it was probably contributing to her feelings of depression. She suggested that Elana try some of the following ideas to help shift her focus to the gifts of the present moment:

1. **Keep a gratitude list.**
   Every day, Elana should write down at least five things that she could be grateful for. She could choose anything, from liking the color of her bedroom to laughing with a friend to getting a good grade. She should hang the list where she would see it all the time.

2. **Plan activities she likes to do.**
   Elana should make a list of daily and weekly activities that she would like to do: listening to music, playing with her dog, watching movies, swimming, or anything else that makes her happy. She should be sure to plan them into her schedule, so that she has something positive to do every day. She needs to balance all the work she does for the future with some fun in the present.

3. **Practice focusing on what she is doing in the present moment.**
   If Elana is eating ice cream, she should really pay attention to its taste, texture, and color, and to how much she is enjoying it. If she is doing homework, she should think about the subject and what interests her about it, not just about the grade she wants to get. If she is riding her bike, she should pay full attention to the experience—the feel of the path, the freedom of the wind in her hair, and the fun of the ride.

4. **Stop her negative focus on the future.**
   If Elana notices herself thinking these thoughts, she should tell herself, "Stop!" and turn her mind to something positive in the present instead.

As Elana put these ideas into practice, she began to enjoy her life more. Nothing had changed outwardly, but inwardly she had let go of her negative future focus.

directions

For the next week, practice the above suggestions in your own life. After seven days, your gratitude list should have thirty-five items on it. Staple or tape your list to this page.

Write a list of the pleasurable activities you can realistically do daily and weekly.

_____

_____

_____

_____

_____

As you go through the coming week, try focusing on the positive gifts of the moment. Describe what this is like for you.

_____

_____

_____

When you find yourself thinking negatively about the future, tell yourself "Stop!" and replace these thoughts with positive thoughts of the present. Write some of those negative thoughts and the positive thoughts that replaced them.

_____

_____

_____

_____

_____

_____

more to do

Describe what it was like trying to shift your focus this week.

_____

_____

_____

Tell which seems more natural to you—focusing on the present moment or thinking about the future—and why.

_____

_____

_____

Tell which is easier for you—focusing on possible negative outcomes or focusing on current positive realities—and why.

_____

_____

_____

Describe a time when one of the above activities helped you feel less depressed.

_____

_____

_____

Tell which activities you plan to use in the future to combat feelings of depression. Explain why you chose those.

_____

_____

_____

10 higher-power help

you need to know

Many people believe that there is a power in the universe that is bigger than themselves. Holding this belief can help them let go of problems and tolerate difficult life situations. It can help them find peace and strength within themselves. If you have a belief in a higher power, it can help you to combat feelings of depression.

The idea of a higher power means different things to different people. People may think of a higher power as spirit, nature, love, or something else. They may call this higher power by different names, although the most common is God.

People who believe in a higher power may belong to an organized religion, such as Christianity, Islam, or Judaism, but you do not have to have any particular religious ideas to believe in a higher power.

If you believe that there is a force in the universe that is more powerful than yourself, you can use your belief to help you combat depression by:

- Tapping in to this power for strength when you feel your human strength is not enough

- Mentally turning over difficult problems to this power, trusting that a positive outcome will occur

- Communicating your concerns to this power through prayer or meditation and asking for help in the problem's resolution

- Believing that this power is responsible for creating an ordered universe and that there is a reason for everything that happens to you, even if you don't understand it at the moment

- Focusing on the peaceful and positive spirit of this power to help you feel peaceful and positive within yourself

directions

In the box below, write or draw or paste anything that helps you describe your personal ideas about a higher power. Give your expression a title.

Title: _____

Describe a situation that you have been feeling depressed about lately. Tell how you could use your belief in a higher power to help you to cope or to feel better.

_____

_____

_____

_____

more to do

Tell how your ideas about a higher power originated. Did you learn them from your family, the media, school, within yourself, or another source?

_____

_____

_____

Tell how you see others using their belief in a higher power to help them cope with life.

_____

_____

_____

Describe a situation you have experienced that confirms your belief in a higher power.

_____

_____

_____

Describe any conflicting feelings you may have about your beliefs.

_____

_____

Make a list of people you know whom you could comfortably discuss your beliefs with. Which of these people might help you use your beliefs to combat depression?

_____

_____

Make a plan or schedule an appointment to talk with one or more of these people within the next week. Tell what you learned from your talk.

_____

_____

healthy self-esteem 11

you need to know

People's self-esteem reflects the manner and degree to which they value themselves. People who have healthy self-esteem see themselves in a positive yet realistic way. People whose self-esteem is not healthy often have an overly negative view of themselves. When you have healthy self-esteem, you are less likely to feel depressed.

Justin's healthy self-esteem allows him to make mistakes and not hate himself or think he is a failure. He knows that he has many strengths, like solving math problems, skateboarding, and fixing cars. He also knows that there are things he needs a lot of help with, like remembering to do his chores, keeping his temper under control, and anything having to do with English class. When Justin got in trouble with his boss at the fast-food restaurant for not cleaning the fry machine two days in a row, he reminded himself that he was doing well in the other areas of his job, but he definitely needed to work on remembering all of his responsibilities. He decided to make a checklist of everything that had to be done before he left each night. By looking at his list, he stopped forgetting the fry machine. He feels good that he solved the problem.

Chase struggles with keeping his self-esteem at a healthy level. Whenever he falls short of his own expectations, he tells himself he is an idiot and has messed up again. Chase is a good student, a good friend, and a hard worker. But he never pays attention to his strengths because he is too busy focusing on his weaknesses. When Chase was accepted into the National Honor Society, his family was proud of him. But Chase felt bad about himself because he was thinking of how he had messed up in a class presentation the day before. When Chase made the baseball team, his friends were happy for him, but he felt bad about himself because he had only made second string, not first. When he feels bad about himself, he also loses the energy to make improvements.

These two boys view themselves in different ways. Justin is more often happy, even when something goes wrong, because he focuses on his strengths and accepts and corrects his weaknesses. Chase is more often depressed, even when something goes right, because his excessive focus on his weaknesses makes him forget all about his strengths. Then he feels too discouraged to try to correct his weaknesses.

directions

Rate your self-esteem on the scale below.

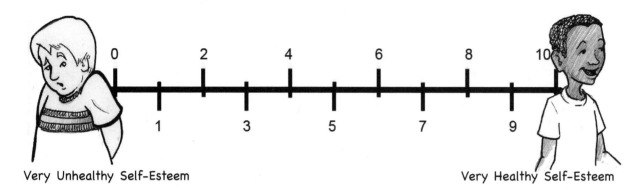

Very Unhealthy Self-Esteem   Very Healthy Self-Esteem

In the left column below, list your inner qualities that you feel are positive; in the right column, list your inner qualities that you feel are negative. These could include anything from the kind of friend you are to being honest or deceptive to having a good sense of humor or being a sore loser.

Positive Inner Qualities	Negative Inner Qualities

List things that you are good at doing in the left column below and list things that you need to improve at doing in the right column. These could include anything from playing soccer to being punctual to cleaning your room or caring for your pet.

Things I Am Good at Doing	Things I Need to Improve at Doing

If you don't have as many items listed in your left (positive) columns as you do in your right (negative) columns, add more. If you can't think of enough by yourself, ask a friend or family member to help you. Don't stop until you have as many items listed in the left columns as in the right.

After looking at your lists, rate your self-esteem again.

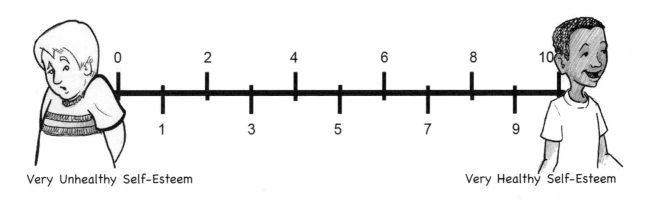

Very Unhealthy Self-Esteem   Very Healthy Self-Esteem

more to do

Explain why you gave yourself the rating you did on the first scale.

_____

_____

Explain any difference between your first and second ratings.

_____

_____

Tell how you think you developed the self-esteem that you have now. From where or from whom did you learn to feel positive or negative about yourself?

_____

_____

Tell how your self-esteem affects whether you feel happy or depressed.

_____

_____

Describe what changes you could make in your view of yourself that would help you have healthier self-esteem.

_____

_____

Describe what it felt like for you to ask other people about your strengths and weaknesses.

_____

_____

Some people think that focusing on their strengths makes them conceited. Being conceited means that you often brag about your strengths to others and you rarely admit to having faults. Healthy self-esteem involves being realistic, which means that you recognize, accept, and admit to both your strengths and your weaknesses.

you need to know

All of us are loved and valued by another person or persons, but we don't always recognize it. When people are aware that they are loved and valued, they tend to feel better about themselves and their life in general. Realizing and confirming that you are loved can help you to combat feelings of depression.

When Kelsey was depressed, she often felt very alone in the world. Even though she had a family and friends, she never felt like her life made a difference to anyone. Her parents were both busy with their jobs and caring for her younger siblings. They didn't spend much time alone with her, and she felt like she just wasn't that important to them. Kelsey had friends to do things with, but she often felt empty after being with them. She felt like she was just another person to hang out with but not of any real value to them for who she was.

When Kelsey told her counselor about this, the counselor said that she understood Kelsey's feelings but she also thought that Kelsey's perception was mistaken. Often people forget to tell or show others that they are loved, but that doesn't mean the love isn't there. The counselor invited Kelsey's parents and two of her friends to the next counseling session. Each person was asked to describe how they felt about Kelsey, and why.

Kelsey's parents said that they loved Kelsey with all their hearts. She was their first-born and would always be special to them. They loved her simply because she was their child, but they also loved things about her, like her gentleness, her sensitivity, her caring for animals, and her sense of humor. They said that no matter what happened, they would love her for as long as they lived.

Kelsey's friends said that they loved Kelsey because she was a good listener and a loyal friend. They knew they could tell Kelsey a secret and she would keep it. They knew that she would be there for them if they ever needed a shoulder to cry on. They said they loved her sweet spirit and her willingness to forgive.

Kelsey was amazed at what she heard. She hadn't realized that her family and friends really valued her in these ways. The counselor said that things aren't always the way we perceive them to be. It is important to check things out with other people rather than assuming we know how they feel. When Kelsey realized that she was loved, she didn't feel as depressed. If she did start to feel sad or lonely, reminding herself that she was loved helped to lift her spirits.

directions

Next to the words below, write the specific names of people in your life who love or value you.

mother	aunt	boyfriend
grandfather	cousin	stepfather
friend at school	sister	teacher
counselor	grandmother	worship leader
girlfriend	uncle	neighborhood friend
brother	father	coach
neighbor	stepmother	friend's parent

Name any other people who love and value you.

_____

_____

_____

Choose two or more of these people to talk to about why they love and value you. Write their reasons here.

_____

_____

_____

_____

_____

_____

_____

more to do

Describe how you felt as you did this exercise, and why.

_____

_____

_____

Tell if you feel that you are loved, and why or why not.

_____

_____

_____

Why do you think that Kelsey didn't realize she was loved?

_____

_____

_____

Describe how feeling loved or not feeling loved is related to any feelings of depression that you have.

_____

_____

_____

It is important to understand that some people have a hard time showing love. Even though they say they love you, it might not seem that way to you. But they may still be loving you in the best way they can.

If you do not feel loved, it is important for you to find someone that you trust to talk to about this. Think of who this would be and schedule a time to talk with that person. If you can't think of anyone, you can ask a school counselor or social worker to help you find someone.

believing in yourself 13

you need to know

People who think that they are victims in a world where they have little or no control are more likely to feel unhappy. Believing in your ability to affect your environment and improve negative situations can eliminate feelings of helplessness. When you know that you can tolerate discomfort and create positive change in your life, you are less likely to become depressed.

Nicole had a hard time handling challenges. When she went to cheerleading tryouts, so many other girls were there that she figured she wouldn't have a chance of making the squad. She immediately gave up the idea of trying out. When she got a low grade on her first art project, she told herself she must not be good in art. She dropped the class even though she had really enjoyed it.

Nicole became discouraged so easily that she never stayed with things long enough to learn that she could get past her initial discomfort. As a result, she never accomplished much and thought of herself as incompetent. She was depressed a lot of the time because she felt like life was very hard and she was a weak victim who could do nothing about it.

Nicole's counselor told her that this was a very strong but false belief. In reality, Nicole was just as able as anyone else to face challenges, accomplish goals, and handle the ups and downs everyone encounters in life. She just didn't believe she could do it, so she gave up before she could prove herself wrong. The counselor told Nicole that it was time to change her thoughts. Believing in herself would give her strength and she would feel less depressed. The counselor suggested that Nicole follow these steps from belief to action:

Have a belief in yourself. Tell yourself that you are just as capable as anyone else. Know that you are stronger than you once thought.

Examine the possibilities. Instead of seeing one closed door, see many other open doors. Think of all the things you can do to change your situation.

Look closely at your choices and pick one to try.

Put your plan into action. Act on your belief in yourself. If your first plan doesn't work, try a second one.

directions

Briefly describe something in your life that is making you feel depressed because you don't believe in your ability to change it.

_____

_____

H: Right now, make a conscious decision to change your thoughts about yourself. Decide to believe that you can make a difference. Copy these words on the line below and sign your name: "I am not helpless. I believe in my ability to handle this."

_____

_____

E: Make a list of all the possible ways you can change this situation.

_____

_____

_____

L: Evaluate all your alternatives and write a plan for when, where, and how you will try making a change.

_____

_____

_____

P: Help yourself by acting on your plan and then describe your results.

_____

_____

_____

more to do

Think about where you might have gotten the idea that you should not believe in yourself or your ability to help yourself. Write about it here.

_____

_____

_____

Describe how your beliefs about yourself contribute to feelings of depression.

_____

_____

_____

Tell whether you wish to continue thinking that you are helpless or unable to accomplish what you want, and why.

_____

_____

Make a list of situations in your life that you could make better by believing in yourself.

_____

_____

_____

Tell why you have just as much ability as anyone else to believe in yourself and to make positive changes in your life.

_____

_____

Remember, the first plan doesn't always work, for anyone. Continue to believe in yourself and try your plans, and eventually you will make a difference. Continue following the plan of H-E-L-P.

14 asserting yourself

you need to know

People who never stand up for their own rights or voice their own opinions often feel hurt, used, or depressed. Standing up for yourself in an appropriate manner is called being assertive. When you are able to act assertively, you are less likely to feel depressed.

Using assertive behavior means that you recognize when you have a need, and you try your best to get it filled through appropriate channels. Appropriate channels are those in which you take action for yourself but do not hurt others in the process. Your inner voice says, "I count, and so do you."

Never standing up for yourself, but then feeling sad or complaining when you don't get what you need, is called passive behavior. If you act passively, you most often let other people tell you what to do. Even if you don't like it, you don't take any direct or healthy steps to change it. You might whine or complain behind other people's backs, but you never assert yourself. As a result, you rarely get your needs met and often feel depressed. Your inner voice says, "I don't count."

Sometimes people think that in order to get their needs met they have to use force. If you recognize your needs and try to fill them but don't care whom you hurt in the process, you are using aggressive behavior. When you act aggressively, you may blame, insult, intimidate, or put down other people to get what you want. You may alienate people or lose friends. While you might look powerful on the outside, on the inside you may actually feel depressed. Your inner voice says, "I count, but you don't."

Learning and using assertive behavior can help you to get your needs met, feel good about yourself, have good relationships with other people, and combat depression.

directions

Read the situations below and the statements to the right of them. Write "passive," "assertive," or "aggressive" below each statement, according to the behavior it illustrates.

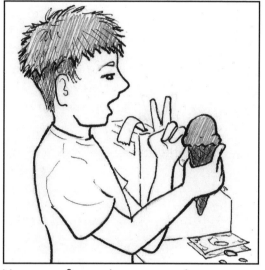

You pay for a two-scoop ice cream cone but only get one scoop.

You say, "Hey, this place is a rip-off!" and smash your cone on the counter.

_____

You say, "Excuse me, but there was a mistake. I paid for two scoops, but you've only given me one."

_____

You say nothing and walk out the door feeling disappointed and angry.

_____

You get a poor grade on a paper you worked very hard on and were proud of.

You approach the teacher and curse. You tell him that your parents are on the school board and he could lose his job for giving you an unfair grade.

_____

You think that you must be dumber than you thought and probably deserve the poor grade.

_____

You approach the teacher and ask if he can meet with you later to discuss your paper. At the meeting you explain how much work you put into it and how surprised you were at receiving the poor grade.

_____

You are working on a group science project. The group is deciding what each member will contribute to the project.

You say, "Let's talk about our strengths and how we can work together to do a good project. I'm good at doing research."

You let someone else tell you what you should do and don't say anything when it's something you are not good at and really don't like to do.

Without asking for input, you tell the group what each will do.

You would like to ask someone to dance but are afraid of rejection.

You walk up to someone who looks friendly and say, "Hi, I was wondering if you'd like to dance."

You stand by the wall, feeling angry that no one is asking you to dance.

You walk over to a group of kids, pull one forcefully by the arm, and say, "Come on, dance with me."

more to do

Tell whether you are most often passive, assertive, or aggressive. _____

Describe anything you may have missed out on by being overly passive.

_____

_____

Tell what you could have done to be assertive instead.

_____

_____

Describe anyone you may have hurt by being overly aggressive.

_____

_____

Tell what you could have done to be assertive instead.

_____

_____

Explain why being assertive might be difficult.

_____

_____

Describe how learning to be assertive could help you to combat depression.

_____

_____

As you go through the next few days, look for chances to practice being assertive. If you are unsure what assertive behavior might be in some situation, ask a counselor or another adult for an opinion.

15 using social skills

you need to know

Being involved in fulfilling relationships is one of the greatest factors contributing to happiness in life. People who have supportive and caring relationships are less likely to feel depressed. Starting and maintaining relationships involves talking to other people, which may feel uncomfortable at first. When you learn a few simple tips for talking to people, it becomes much easier to form, keep, and enjoy relationships.

Using good manners means speaking and acting in ways that are polite, friendly, and respectful of others. For example, if you are at your first student council meeting, you smile, say hello to people, and listen to others without interrupting. If you are asking someone if you can borrow some notebook paper, you say please and thank you and return some paper to them as soon as you can. If you accidentally bump into someone in the hallway, you say, "Excuse me." You treat others the way you would like to be treated yourself.

Having integrity means choosing actions that are sincere, honest, and honorable. For example, if you see someone drop a $5 bill while buying lunch in the cafeteria, you pick it up and give it back. You do your own work in class without looking at others' papers, and you don't talk about people behind their backs. Again, you treat others the way you would like to be treated yourself.

When you use good manners and have integrity, other people will feel that you respect them. This helps them to develop a feeling of trust for you and makes them enjoy being around you. It makes them want to treat you with respect as well.

directions

In the pictures below, all of the kids are using poor social skills. Write what they should be doing differently to use good manners and integrity.

1. _____
   _____
   _____
   _____
   _____
   _____
   _____
   _____
   _____

2. _____
   _____
   _____
   _____
   _____
   _____
   _____
   _____

3. _____

4. _____

more to do

Look back at the pictures once more. For each situation, explain why you would or would not enjoy the main character's company.

Picture 1: _____

_____

_____

Picture 2: _____

_____

_____

Picture 3: _____

_____

_____

Picture 4: _____

_____

_____

Think about your own behavior in social situations. If it is difficult to determine your own good or poor social skills, ask someone who knows you well to give you input. Then make a list of the social skills you use that would make people enjoy being around you.

_____

_____

_____

_____

Make a list of your behaviors that might make people not enjoy being around you.

_____

_____

_____

_____

Think even more closely about your behavior. Describe how your social skills might affect the quality of your relationships with your friends, family members, or acquaintances.

_____

_____

_____

How does the quality of your relationships affect your feelings of depression?

_____

_____

_____

Describe specifically what you could do to speak or act in a way that could improve the quality of your relationships and make people enjoy being around you more.

_____

_____

_____

Over the next few days, try out some of the behaviors you just described. Tell what happens.

_____

_____

_____

talking tips from AL 16

you need to know

Being involved in fulfilling relationships is one of the greatest factors contributing to happiness in life. People who have supportive and caring relationships are less likely to feel depressed. Starting and maintaining relationships involves talking to other people, which may feel uncomfortable at first. When you learn a few simple tips for talking to people, it becomes much easier to form, keep, and enjoy relationships.

School was starting in two weeks, and Rob noticed himself feeling depressed again. He felt that way every year because he started thinking about meeting new kids. He never knew what to say to people, which made him feel bad about himself. Usually he ended up saying nothing. He knew this was one of the reasons he didn't have many friends, and that made him feel depressed, too.

Rob's older brother, Al, noticed him looking sad and asked what was wrong. Rob didn't want to tell him at first because he thought Al would make fun of him. Al was in college, and he was so confident about everything that Rob figured he would just laugh at him.

But Al didn't laugh. In fact, he said he knew exactly how Rob felt because he used to feel the same way. Al said he had learned to be comfortable talking with people by remembering two words that started with the letters in his name. The first word was ASK, and the second word was LISTEN. He described what he called the "AL method."

"When you can't think of anything to say, just ask people a question about themselves," Al explained. "It makes them feel good that you are interested in them, and it gives you something to talk about. After you ask, listen carefully to their answers. Look into their eyes when they talk to you, and make a thoughtful comment about what they said. It is a real compliment to people when you listen to them carefully. It shows kindness and respect, and people appreciate that."

Rob noticed that the AL method didn't really involve much talking on his part, so he thought he might be able to do it. When he tried, he discovered that his brother was right. Asking people a question about themselves created a conversation right away. He could keep the conversation going by asking more questions about what they had answered. He noticed that when he listened carefully, it made people happy. It also gave him information to ask more questions about. As Rob got better and better at the AL method, he found himself feeling less depressed. In fact, he actually started looking forward to talking to people.

directions

Try the AL method yourself. In each of the pictures on the next page, label one speaker with your name and the other with the name of someone you would like to talk to. Underneath the picture, write where you might be when you talk to this person. Then write a question that you could ask this person, an answer that they might give, and a thoughtful comment that you could make after listening carefully to what they've said. You can use the picture below as an example.

Where you might be: **at a swim meet**

Where you might be:

_____

Where you might be:

_____

more to do

Describe how you usually feel when you have to make conversation with others, and why.

_____

_____

Practice thinking of questions you could ask people about themselves. Write two questions you could ask each person below to start a conversation.

Someone who is standing at your school bus stop

1. _____

2. _____

Someone who has been assigned to do a history project with you

1. _____

2. _____

Someone whose locker is next to yours

1. _____

2. _____

Someone who is standing next to you in the cafeteria line

1. _____

2. _____

Someone who is sitting next to you in the bleachers at a basketball game

1. _____

2. _____

Tell how your ability to talk to other people affects your level of depression.

_____

_____

_____

Over the next twenty-four hours, practice the AL method. Whenever you talk to someone, ask an appropriate question about that person and then listen carefully to the answer. In the chart below, write the name of the person you talked to, the question you asked, and the answer.

Name	Question	Answer

good communication skills 17

you need to know

Good communication skills involve not only what people say, but also their attitude when they speak and how they look and sound. People with good communication skills are more likely to maintain fulfilling relationships, so they are less likely to feel depressed. If these skills don't come naturally to you, you can learn them.

Many of us think of communication as something we do only through our speech. What we say does express our ideas, but we also communicate by the way we look, the way we sound, and our attitude.

Looks

The way we hold our body and the look on our face express a great deal about our thoughts and feelings. If someone says the words, "I love you," in a fighting stance with fists up, eyebrows furrowed, and teeth bared, we will probably not believe the person's words. If you want to have a positive relationship with someone, it is best to present yourself using open and relaxed, rather than aggressive, body language.

Sound

The way we use our voice when we speak can tell other people about the feelings behind our words. A loud or intense voice usually expresses more aggression than a quiet or calm one. Speaking very quickly can express urgency, while speaking slowly can express peacefulness. If you want to have a positive relationship with someone, it is best to present yourself using an open and relaxed, rather than aggressive, voice.

Attitude

A positive relationship is best created by using a positive and accepting attitude rather than a negative or critical attitude. Here are some ways to achieve this:

- Use "I feel" statements. For example, instead of saying, "You have such a big mouth!" say, "I feel hurt when I learn that you have shared information I trusted you to keep to yourself." Or instead of saying, "You can forget about ever going to the movies with me again!" say, "I feel angry when we make plans to go to the movies and then you cancel at the last minute."

- Differentiate between people and their actions. For example, instead of saying, "I hate you!" say, "I hate what you did." Instead of saying, "You're such a pig," say, "Some of your eating habits are really rude."

- Be open to accepting other points of view. For example, instead of saying, "You can't seriously believe that!" say, "That is really different from the way I think about things." Or instead of saying, "You are totally wrong," say, "I don't think I agree with you, but tell me how you see it."

directions

Draw a line from the criticisms and attacks on the left to the corresponding "I feel" statements and descriptions of behavior on the right.

"You are so nosy."

"It's taking you a long time to understand this; let me think of another way to explain it."

"You STILL don't get it? Man, are you dumb!"

"Could you please take your soda cans out of my car?"

"I can't stand people like you."

"When you stand that close to me, I feel like you're in my personal space."

"Get out of my face, would you?"

"When you go through my backpack without asking me, I feel like my privacy has been invaded."

"You are such a slob."

"When you act that way, I feel really angry."

In the box below, draw pictures or tape magazine pictures or photographs of people who are expressing their feelings in their faces and their bodies. Underneath each picture, write how their appearance communicates their thoughts and feelings.

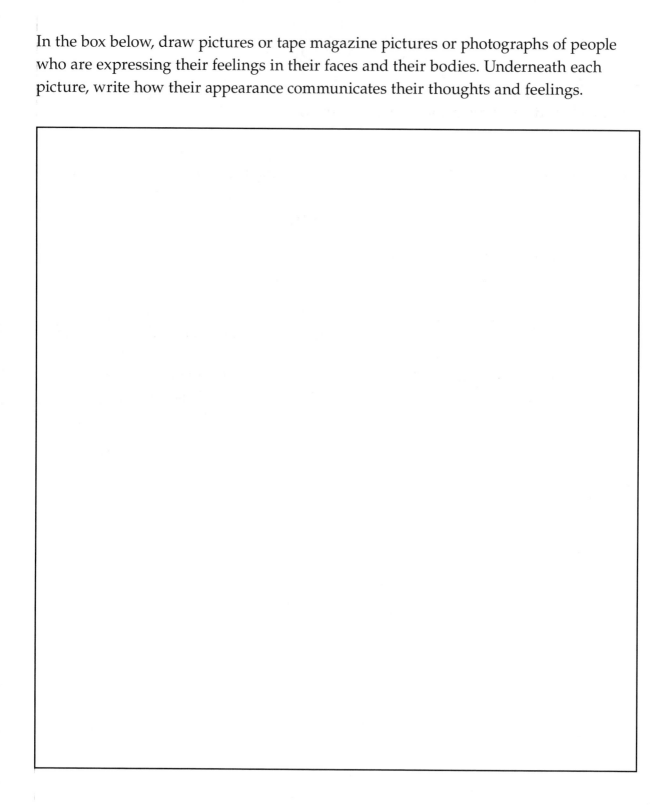

more to do

The next time you are in front of a mirror in private, practice arranging your face and your body in different ways. Try to see the difference between a look that is open and calm and a look that is aggressive. Decide which look would help you communicate in the most positive way with other people. Describe it here.

_____

_____

_____

Next, practice using your voice with different degrees of loudness, different tones and pitches, and speaking at different rates. If possible, use a tape recorder to help you. Listen closely to the way your voice sounds, and think about whether it gives off a negative or positive feeling. Decide which intonations and patterns would help you to communicate in the most positive way with other people. Describe them here.

_____

_____

_____

Think about specific problems you have had in relationships. Describe how your attitude may have contributed to the problem.

_____

_____

_____

_____

_____

Tell how you can adjust your attitude to be more accepting of others.

_____

_____

_____

_____

_____

_____

Describe how your communication skills might contribute to your feelings of depression.

_____

_____

_____

_____

_____

_____

Tell how improving your communication skills might help relieve your feelings of depression.

_____

_____

_____

_____

_____

_____

managing conflict and disagreements 18

you need to know

People who have trouble managing conflict are more likely to feel depressed. Their relationships are usually more difficult and less fulfilling and tend not to last. It is normal for people to disagree with each other, but when you know healthy ways to manage those disagreements, your relationships can be more peaceful and bring you more happiness.

Derrick and Haley had a lot in common. They were both in the yearbook club, both liked science fiction movies and cheese-only pizza, and both had nearly the same class schedule at school. They spent a lot of time together, but they had frequent arguments. They seemed to fight about little things, and their arguments became big very quickly. Sometimes they would have a disagreement and not talk for days. This would make each of them feel lonely and depressed.

When the new semester started, both Derrick and Haley were in a class called "Interpersonal Communications." One of the first subjects the teacher introduced was conflict management. She gave the class a list of guidelines that would help people resolve conflicts in a healthy and productive way. Derrick and Haley looked at the list. These were some of the guidelines:

1. When you find yourself in an emotionally heated argument, stop. People cannot think clearly or solve problems when they are not calm. Schedule a time to discuss your situation objectively, when you will be relaxed, cooled down, and not hurried or tired.

2. Agree on a clear, specific definition of the problem. See it as something outside of yourselves, rather than as a flaw in either one of you. See yourselves as a team whose goal is to solve the problem. Think of ways to attack the problem instead of attacking each other.

3. Agree to treat each other with respect, not using negative or insulting terms ("idiot," "jerk," etc.). Agree not to blame or criticize.

4. Focus on only one topic at a time, only on the present situation, and not on past problems. (Say, "Today I felt irritated when you were twenty minutes late" rather than, "You can never get anywhere on time. Remember last week?")

5. Agree to listen to each other, even if you don't agree with what is being said. Respect each other's right to have different opinions.

6. Focus on the different perspectives in the way you see things, not the impact of the problem. ("I think foreign films are challenging; you think they are confusing" rather than, "I hate going to the movies with you.")

7. Think in terms of negotiation and compromise rather than winning and losing.

Derrick and Haley realized that they currently did many of the things these guidelines said not to do. They kept arguing as they got more and more upset, they called each other names and blamed the problem on the other person, they nearly always brought up past arguments, and each of them had a strong desire to "win" the argument. As they began to practice the new conflict management guidelines, their disagreements began ending much more quickly. They started trying to find solutions together rather than each of them trying to be the only winner. They also noticed their relationships with other friends were improving as well. After a few months, both Derrick and Haley felt much happier about their friendship, themselves, and life in general.

directions

Over the next few days, listen to your friends and family members or to people on television as they have disagreements. Use the forms below to keep track of the actions they take that either increase the conflict or help manage the conflict.

Names: _____

Topic of disagreement: _____

Discussing while emotionally heated or calm? _____

Working as a team or attacking? _____

Treating with respect or disrespect? _____

Sticking to one topic in the present? _____

Listening carefully to each other? _____

Identifying different perspectives? _____

Negotiating or trying to win? _____

Names: _____

Topic of disagreement: _____

Discussing while emotionally heated or calm? _____

Working as a team or attacking? _____

Treating with respect or disrespect? _____

Sticking to one topic in the present? _____

Listening carefully to each other? _____

Identifying different perspectives? _____

Negotiating or trying to win? _____

Names: _____

Topic of disagreement: _____

Discussing while emotionally heated or calm? _____

Working as a team or attacking? _____

Treating with respect or disrespect? _____

Sticking to one topic in the present? _____

Listening carefully to each other? _____

Identifying different perspectives? _____

Negotiating or trying to win? _____

Names: _____

Topic of disagreement: _____

Discussing while emotionally heated or calm? _____

Working as a team or attacking? _____

Treating with respect or disrespect? _____

Sticking to one topic in the present? _____

Listening carefully to each other? _____

Identifying different perspectives? _____

Negotiating or trying to win? _____

more to do

Look back over the notes you took as you watched people disagree. For each disagreement you observed, describe the specific words and actions you noticed that increased the conflict and those that helped to manage it:

1. _____

   _____

2. _____

   _____

3. _____

   _____

4. _____

   _____

Think about yourself and your own actions during disagreements. Tell which actions you take most often that help to increase conflict.

_____

_____

Tell which actions you take most often that help to manage conflict.

_____

_____

Tell how the amount of conflict in your relationships affects your level of happiness or depression.

_____

Tell what you can practice doing to better manage conflict in your relationships.

_____

19 problem-solving skills

you need to know

No one has a life without problems. People who feel capable of facing the challenges that life presents are less likely to feel depressed. They know that they can solve problems, and they put their skills to work when challenges arise. You can increase your problem-solving skills by learning and practicing a five-step plan.

Joshua felt depressed a lot. There always seemed to be something going wrong in his life. Class assignments were too hard; friends didn't return his calls; his boss at the convenience store said he daydreamed too much. When those things cleared up, other things went wrong. Joshua shared his frustration with his counselor at school. The counselor said all of the things that bothered Joshua were problems that could be solved. But Joshua said he didn't have any idea of how to solve them.

The counselor told Joshua that there were five steps he could follow to help him find solutions to his current problems or any others that might come along. She wrote these steps on her notepad and then explained each one, using Joshua's first challenge as an example.

Step 1: Clearly define the problem.
The counselor said that people have a better chance of changing something when they know exactly what it is that needs to change. Instead of just saying that class assignments are too hard, Joshua could think more carefully about what made them difficult. Joshua said he never felt he understood the assignments clearly. After he turned them in, the teacher often said that he hadn't followed the directions. The counselor then defined the problem more clearly by writing, "Have trouble understanding exactly what the teacher wants from me."

Step 2: Brainstorm solutions.
Next the counselor asked Joshua to tell her all the possible solutions that he could think of to that problem, no matter how crazy or far-fetched they sounded. Joshua came up with these ideas:

Listen more carefully when the assignment is explained.

Ask a friend to reexplain it to me after class.

Use a tape-recorder to tape the teacher's explanation of the assignment.

Ask if I can have a different teacher.

Talk with the teacher and see if I understand the assignment correctly before I start.

Drop out of school so I don't have to do homework at all.

Sit closer to the front of the classroom.

Step 3: Choose one solution and try it.
Joshua and his counselor went over every item on the list, and Joshua decided to try "Ask a friend to reexplain it to me after class."

Step 4: Evaluate how well it worked.
Joshua tried his plan the next time he got an assignment, but he still didn't do very well. He realized that he wasn't confident his friend had understood what the teacher wanted.

Step 5: If it worked well, keep doing it. If not, try another solution from the list.
Joshua decided to try another idea: "Talk with the teacher and see if I understand the assignment correctly before I start." He did this the next day, and he ended up getting a much better grade on his homework.

As Joshua used this method with other challenges in his life, he found himself feeling more confident in his ability to solve problems. Life didn't feel as depressing anymore.

directions

Name a problem that you have been facing lately. _____

_____

Write a clear and concise definition of the problem so that you know exactly what you need to work on. _____

_____

_____

Brainstorm possible solutions to your problem. For brainstorming to be most effective, it is important that you write down all the ideas that come into your head, without judging them. It doesn't matter how unusual or impossible they may be; write them down anyway. Make your list as long as possible. If you need more space than is provided here, use additional paper.

_____

_____

_____

_____

_____

_____

_____

_____

_____

_____

_____

Look back over your list. Now think about which ideas are possible or realistic and which are not. Choose one of your ideas to try as a solution to your problem and write it here. Tell when you plan to try this solution.

_____

_____

After you have tried this idea, describe how well it worked. Has this solution solved the problem?

_____

_____

_____

If this idea didn't work, choose another solution from your list and try that. Describe your results here. Continue trying solutions until you find one that works.

_____

_____

_____

_____

more to do

For each of the categories below, draw an arrow to the number on the scale that best describes how confident you feel solving problems in that area.

Look back at the numbers you have chosen and tell why you think some areas may be harder for you to deal with than others.

_____

_____

_____

_____

Describe how your personal ability to solve problems in your life affects your feelings of depression.

_____

_____

_____

_____

Make a list of other problems that are currently challenging you.

_____

_____

_____

_____

Choose one item on your list and follow the five problem-solving steps to deal with it. Record your data and experiences below.

_____

_____

_____

_____

_____

_____

_____

_____

_____

_____

_____

Be aware that you will never stop having challenges in your life. But if you continue to practice your problem-solving skills, the challenges will become easier to handle and you will become more confident in your ability to manage them. This can greatly reduce your feelings of depression.

20 act on the A's to manage stress

you need to know

Most people feel stress almost on a daily basis. When you do not know how to manage stress, it is easy to feel depressed, because you often feel anxious, tired, or overwhelmed. Learning stress-management techniques can help you ward off feelings of depression.

Anna was a straight-A student. She was good at art, acting, accounting, and archery. But Anna was awful at managing stress. Her brain and body always felt overloaded, as if she were running a race that she could never win. This made her feel depressed as well.

One day her Uncle Alex taught Anna the reminder "Act on the A's." Uncle Alex explained that there are three ways to act on stress that all begin with A:

1. **A**void it. Remove yourself from stressful situations when you can; do not purposely put yourself into situations that you know are highly stressful for you; do not dwell on thoughts that raise your stress level.

2. Make **A**djustments. Do what you can to change the stressful situation.

3. **A**lter your thinking. If you can't change something, change your thoughts about it so you don't perceive it as so stressful. Or change the way you cope with it so you can handle it better.

For example, Anna loved art, but it also caused her stress. Her private lessons took up a lot of time in her already busy schedule; she compared herself to others in the class and felt she was not a very good artist; and she worried both about getting into art school and the chances of finding a well-paying job in this very competitive field.

Anna tried to act on the A's. She thought about avoiding art altogether, but she knew she didn't want to do that because she enjoyed it so much She thought about making adjustments and realized she could cut back on her painting lessons or drop archery to give her more time. She decided that art was more important to her, so she dropped archery.

Then she thought about how she could alter her thinking. She decided to stop comparing herself to others in her class; it didn't help her and only made her feel stressed. She also decided to stop worrying about the future. If she didn't make it as a professional artist, she could still paint as a hobby and enjoy it just as much.

Anna's changes gave her a lot more time. She didn't feel as pressured and she found herself enjoying her painting time more than before. Her stress level went down, and her feelings of depression subsided.

directions

Pretend that two of your best friends have come to you with the problems described below. Read about their situations and then write a suggestion about how they can better manage their stress by acting on the A's.

Charyse has so much to do and so little time to do it. Charyse likes to be in charge of things and takes on a lot of responsibilities. She always tries to get good grades, she is the president of two clubs at school, she is the group leader of her science project, she is in charge of the school recycling project, and she babysits for two neighbors whenever they ask her. Sometimes Charyse gets so tired of having everyone count on her that she becomes depressed and feels like running away. She can't see any other way to get away from the stress.

Suggest what Charyse can do to:

Avoid stress _____

_____

Make **A**djustments _____

_____

Alter her thinking _____

_____

Jack is stressed because he feels pressured about smoking. Jack's grandfather, whom he was very close to, died painfully from lung cancer, and Jack has vowed he would never smoke cigarettes. But now some of the guys he hangs around with are smoking, and they are giving him a hard time for not joining them. Jack doesn't want to lose his friends but he really doesn't want to smoke. He has started having trouble sleeping at night because he dreads going to school to be confronted by the situation.

Suggest what Jack can do to:

Avoid stress _____

_____

Make **A**djustments _____

_____

Alter his thinking _____

_____

more to do

Make a list of the things in your own life that feel stressful to you. Put them in order from most to least stressful.

_____

_____

_____

_____

_____

_____

_____

_____

_____

Fill in the blanks below with the first three items on your list. Then write how you can act on the A's in each situation to help yourself manage the stress.

Situation 1: _____

I can **A**void: _____

I can **A**djust: _____

I can **A**lter: _____

Situation 2: _____

I can **A**void: _____

I can **A**djust: _____

I can **A**lter: _____

Situation 3: _____

I can **A**void: _____

I can **A**djust: _____

I can **A**lter: _____

Describe how your stress level affects your feelings of depression.

_____

_____

_____

_____

Try putting the ideas you listed above into action. Describe your results.

_____

_____

_____

_____

21 looking beyond the battle

you need to know

When people feel they are in a depressing situation, they are often so focused on their discomfort that they forget that the situation is only temporary. When you can look "beyond the battle" and remember that whatever you are dealing with will get better with time, you can focus on brighter times ahead and feel less depressed.

When Ty missed his lay-up shot and the basketball team ended up losing the game, he felt terrible. He was embarrassed, disappointed, and depressed. He kept picturing himself missing the shot over and over again.

When Mareesa sprained her ankle and couldn't perform in the dance recital, she felt as if her life was over. She kept thinking about how unlucky she was and how bad the pain was, and she found herself feeling more and more depressed.

When Jonathan asked a girl to the homecoming dance and she said she was already going with someone else, he felt so depressed. It had taken a lot of courage to ask her, and now it was all for nothing. He felt like he would never get over his disappointment.

These kids are feeling depressed because they are focusing on the negative experience in the present. If they looked beyond the present battle, they would realize that their situations are only temporary. For example, Ty will have many more basketball games this season, and his team has a good chance of winning many times. Mareesa's ankle will heal, and she will be able to perform in the next semester's recital. Jonathan will start to think about something else, and he can ask the girl out again after homecoming or find another girl that he likes.

directions

Read the list of situations below that could bring up feelings of depression. Put a check mark next to any that you have experienced. Underneath each situation, write what you could tell yourself that would help you look beyond the battle and feel less depressed.

☐ You find out you have a huge research paper due in only two weeks. _____

_____

_____

☐ You see that the only seat left on the bus is in the very back, and sitting that far back makes you feel nauseated. _____

_____

☐ When you arrive at work, you learn that someone has called in sick and you will have to do their work as well as your own that day. _____

_____

☐ You've practiced really hard all week, but the coach only puts you in the game for five minutes. _____

_____

☐ You planned to spend your birthday money on video games, but you lose your history book and have to use your money to pay for that instead. _____

_____

_____

☐ You're listening to your parents have an argument—again. _____

_____

_____

more to do

Describe a situation that happened to you recently where you could have let go of depressive feelings by looking beyond the battle.

_____

_____

_____

Tell why it might be hard to look beyond the battle in some situations.

_____

_____

_____

Describe a challenging situation that is coming up for you in the near future, where looking beyond the battle could help you to avoid becoming depressed.

_____

_____

_____

Write the words you could tell yourself about this situation to help you to look beyond the battle.

_____

_____

_____

Close your eyes for a minute and picture yourself in this upcoming situation. Notice everything as you imagine it will happen. Then picture yourself saying what you need to in order to look beyond the battle and not feel depressed. Affirm that this is something you will be able to do to help yourself when the time comes.

coping with change

you need to know

It is normal for people to experience some feelings of discomfort when faced with life events that bring about change. Even when change is positive, adjusting to it takes time and energy. When you can learn healthy ways to cope with change, discomfort will pass more quickly instead of turning into depression.

As long as you are alive, you will experience change. It is a normal part of being human. The world is designed to change; seasons change, weather changes, all living things grow and develop and change over the course of their lives.

While adjusting to change is possible, it involves thinking and acting in new ways, which requires time and energy. When you are aware that you need this extra time and energy, you can understand that adjusting to change doesn't happen immediately. Although this may make you uncomfortable for a while, this feeling is normal and will pass. In the meantime, you can focus on helping yourself through the transition.

Practicing any of the healthy coping actions below can help you through a time of change. Some preserve and create energy; some release depressive feelings, which require energy to hold inside.

Healthy Coping Actions

Getting enough sleep (creates energy)

Eating healthy foods (creates energy)

Getting fresh air (creates energy)

Getting physical exercise (creates energy and releases depression)

Expressing your feelings by talking or writing (releases depression)

Focusing on the positive in yourself and the situation (releases depression)

Reminding yourself things will eventually get better (releases depression)

Participating in fun activities (releases depression)

Laughing (creates energy and releases depression)

directions

Record your current age at the right end of the timeline below. Then record all of the major events you have experienced in your life by marking them along the timeline at the appropriate place. These events might include starting a new school, the birth of a sibling, moving to a new home, a parent's divorce, a long illness, a special birthday, a graduation, or anything that has felt like a major life event to you.

⟵―――――――――――――――――――――――――――⟶

Birth   Your Current Age

Tell which of these events created the most change in your life and which created the least change.

Created Most Change   **Created Least Change**

_____   _____

Tell which of these events was the easiest for you to cope with and which was the hardest.

Easiest to Cope With   **Hardest to Cope With**

_____   _____

Tell which of these events brought up the most feelings of depression for you and which brought up the least.

Brought Up the Most Depression   **Brought Up the Least Depression**

_____   _____

more to do

Choose the most recent life event from your timeline. Describe how you used, or could have used, each of the coping actions to help yourself through it.

Event: _____

Sleep: _____

Healthy foods: _____

Fresh air: _____

Exercise: _____

Expression of feelings: _____

_____

Focusing on the positives: _____

Thinking of what will it be like when things get better: _____

_____

Fun activities: _____

_____

Laughter: _____

Think of a life event that is coming up for you in the near future. Describe how you can use each of the coping actions to help yourself through this.

Event: _____

Sleep: _____

Healthy foods: _____

Fresh air: _____

Exercise: _____

Expression of feelings: _____

_____

Focusing on the positives: _____

Thinking of what will it be like when things get better: _____

_____

Fun activities: _____

_____

Laughter: _____

Record your current age at the far left of the timeline below. Along the timeline, record any major events that you may encounter during the next ten years of your life. Tell what coping actions you think you might use to help yourself through them.

⬅———————————————————————————————➡

Your Current Age   Ten Years from Now

_____

_____

_____

_____

_____

_____

_____

rejection, dejection, and trying again 23

you need to know

Everyone experiences loss in many ways throughout the course of life. Both big and small losses occur every day. People who have a hard time handling loss may have more depressive feelings than those who handle it better. You can learn ways to cope with loss to help you manage feelings of depression.

Rejection comes to us in many ways. We are rejected when someone we want to be friends with doesn't want to be friends with us. We are rejected when we try out for a team or a role in a play and don't make it. We are rejected when we ask someone out on a date and that person says no. We are rejected when we apply for a job or to a school and are turned down.

Rejection, which is something that happens to us, doesn't have to mean dejection, which is a way we feel. Being rejected is an act. Feeling dejected, or depressed, is the feeling we choose to respond with. While we may not have control over being rejected, we do have control over our reaction. When we react with less dejection, we have the energy to try again.

Feeling dejected following rejection is based on the mistaken belief that we have to feel unhappy when we don't get what we want. However, there is more than one road to happiness, and often there is something even better out there waiting for us. When we understand this, we can view rejection more objectively, and we don't have to feel so depressed. Instead of thinking, "I didn't get what I wanted, and if I can't have that, I can't be happy," we can think, "I didn't get what I wanted, but maybe there is something else that can make me happy, too—and maybe even happier than the first thing!" This gives us the encouragement and the energy to try again. When we keep trying, we are usually successful eventually.

directions

The kids in the pictures below have been rejected and are feeling dejected. Write thoughts that could help them see things more objectively. Then write what might happen if they try again.

1. This girl didn't make the cheerleading squad.

1. _____
_____
_____
_____
_____
_____
_____

2. This boy didn't get crowned homecoming king.

2. _____
_____
_____
_____
_____
_____
_____

3. This girl didn't get accepted to National Honor Society.

3. _____
_____
_____
_____
_____
_____
_____
_____
_____

4. This boy didn't get asked to a party.

4. _____
_____
_____
_____
_____
_____
_____
_____

more to do

Why do you think rejection hurts so much? _____

_____

_____

_____

Make a list of rejections you have had in your life. _____

_____

_____

_____

Tell whether your thoughts about each of these rejections made you feel dejected or not._____

_____

_____

Tell if any of these rejections ever resulted in your getting something better than you originally wanted. _____

_____

_____

Some now-famous authors whose work was originally rejected by publishing houses include Stephen King (*Carrie, The Dark Tower*), F. Scott Fitzgerald (*The Great Gatsby*), Anne Frank (*The Diary of Anne Frank*), William Golding (*Lord of the Flies*), Ernest Hemingway (*The Old Man and the Sea*), Joseph Heller (*Catch-22*), Beatrix Potter (*The Tale of Peter Rabbit*), Herman Melville (*Moby Dick*), Edgar Allan Poe (*The Raven*), Dr. Seuss (*The Cat in the Hat*), and H. G. Wells (*The Time Machine, War of the Worlds*).

If you have been rejected, you are in good company. Think of what the world would have missed if these authors had been too depressed to try again.

coping with loss 24

you need to know

Everyone experiences rejection at some time in life. Being rejected can cause many people to feel dejected or depressed. Learning to view rejection objectively helps you to realize you don't have to feel depressed. You can have the courage to try again.

As long as we are alive and growing, we will experience loss. For example, when you graduate from grade school, you lose your place in that school and must move on to another one. When you learn how to drive, you lose some dependency on your parents. When you go steady with one person, you lose the freedom to date other people.

During adolescence, there are a number of normal losses that can occur. These include the loss of grandparents and pets to death from old age, or the loss of peers to death from accidents. There is the loss of your childhood and your child's body. There is the loss of relationships when childhood friends move away or go to other schools or join different groups of friends. There may also be the loss of family stability due to parents' illness or divorce.

It is normal for people to go through a grieving process when they experience loss. Grief may be brief or extended, depending on the importance of what is lost. Grief can involve periods of sadness or depression mixed with periods of confusion, anger, or even happiness. It is important to understand that grief is normal, and each person going through it experiences its progression a little differently.

Keep in mind the following guidelines to help you cope with grief and loss:

- Know that your feelings are normal. It is typical to have many different feelings when you experience a loss. For example, you may feel happy to graduate from one school, sad to say good-bye to this time in your life, scared of what the future will hold, excited at the possibilities, and confused about what choices you will make. If your grandfather dies, you may be sad because you miss him, angry because you didn't want him to leave you, and relieved that he is no longer sick.

- Find a place to express your feelings. Holding all these emotions inside can create body aches and tension or depression. Find a friend, relative, or counselor to share your feelings with, or write them out in a journal or through poetry. Some people express feelings by playing music or even playing sports.

- Continue daily living. Try to stay on a regular schedule of eating, exercise, and sleep. Grieving can be emotionally and physically draining, and you need to maintain your health and energy level to continue with your life and manage your feelings, too.

- Keep linking objects. Look for tangible things that you can keep close at hand to "link" you to what you have lost. If someone has moved away or died, you might keep photographs, letters, articles of clothing, a special book, gift, key chain, or something else that belonged to that person. If you have graduated from high school, you can keep your diploma, yearbooks, pictures, pennants, and other souvenirs from your school experience.

- Plan a ritual or create a memorial. Doing something special to recognize the change can help people move through the grieving process. A party or ceremony ritualizes birthdays, religious accomplishments, graduations, and other growth markers. Planting a tree, engraving a park bench, or creating a memory book are ways to memorialize someone who has died.

directions

In the frame below, draw a picture, make a collage, create a poem, or write about a loss you have experienced recently. Give your creation a title. If you haven't written about it within the frame, describe what happened on the lines underneath.

List any other losses you experienced during adolescence or before.

_____

_____

_____

more to do

On a scale from 1 to 10, with 1 being the most minor loss you have ever experienced and 10 being the most major, assign a number to the loss you described above. Tell what number you chose, and why.

_____

_____

On a scale from 1 to 10, with 1 being the least depressed you have ever felt and 10 being the most depressed, assign a number to your level of depression in relation to this loss. Tell what number you chose, and why.

_____

_____

Make a list of any other feelings you experienced as a result of this loss.

_____

_____

Tell how and where you expressed these feelings. If you haven't yet expressed them, describe them here.

_____

_____

_____

Describe how your daily eating, sleeping, or exercise habits were affected by this loss.

_____

_____

_____

Describe any linking objects you have that did or could help you through this loss.

_____

_____

_____

Describe any rituals you did or could perform to help you cope with this loss.

_____

_____

_____

Describe anything you could have done or could still do to help you through the grieving process over this loss. Tell when you plan to do these things for yourself.

_____

_____

_____

_____

25 getting outside yourself

you need to know

Feelings of depression tend to grow when people dwell on their own problems. Focusing away from yourself, or getting "outside" yourself, can help you feel better. One effective way to do this is to focus on helping someone else who is in need.

Chantelle felt depressed because she was lonely. Even in a crowd of people, she often felt as if she had no friends. She just didn't feel connected to anyone. When she joined the Service Over Self Club at school, Chantelle was asked to help at different places in the community that needed volunteers. One week she read stories to children who were in the cancer unit of the hospital. The next week she and the other club members sang holiday songs at the senior citizens' home. The week after that Chantelle collected canned goods and clothing for people whose homes had been destroyed by a hurricane.

Each time Chantelle came home from a club project, she found herself feeling less lonely inside. She realized that during the time she had been helping other people, she had stopped thinking about her own feelings of depression. She realized that many people were in worse situations than she was, and she felt good because she could do something to help. She also found that she liked interacting with the people she helped. They were always so glad to see her.

As Chantelle continued to do volunteer work, her spirits lifted and she wasn't as depressed. She also began reaching out to other kids at school. She found herself genuinely caring about other people, talking and laughing with them more, and feeling more connected to both her old and new friends.

directions

Think of someone you know who is hurting in some way, needs help with something, or needs cheering up. It might be a friend, family member, neighbor, school staff person, or anyone you know. Think of an act of kindness you could do for that person in the week ahead. Could you help with a chore? Send a card or an encouraging note? Buy that person a soda or cup of coffee? Listen to him or her? Write your ideas here.

_____

_____

_____

Plan to carry out your idea. Tell when and how you will do this.

_____

_____

_____

After you have carried out your plan, describe what happened.

_____

_____

_____

How often did you think about your own feelings of depression while you were planning and carrying out this act of kindness?

_____

_____

How did you feel after you gave this gift of yourself?

_____

_____

more to do

The activities listed below provide a number of opportunities for getting outside yourself and helping other people. Circle any that sound interesting to you.

tutoring children	giving blood	delivering meals to homebound people
reading to the blind	babysitting	writing to people in prison
collecting recyclables	visiting seniors	teaching English to foreigners
doing office work	making phone calls	visiting people in hospitals
delivering library books	cleaning houses	making lunches for the homeless
raising money	having a bake sale	mowing lawns
painting houses	assisting teachers	writing to soldiers
planning events	doing walk-a-thons	working with the disabled
building houses	coaching sports	serving food
caring for animals	translating	answering a crisis hotline
being a tour guide	stuffing envelopes	cooking meals
being a camp counselor	playing in a band	preparing first-aid kits

List any other volunteer activities that you would like to try.

_____

_____

_____

_____

Circle any of the skills or talents in the list below that you could teach to others.

sewing	reading	drawing
cooking	making jewelry	singing
painting	playing chess	taking photographs
playing cards	writing	using a computer
riding a bike	swimming	skateboarding
gardening	crafts	playing tennis
keyboarding	woodworking	scrapbooking
knitting	doing math	playing an instrument
baking	interior decorating	writing poetry
dancing	playing basketball	caring for pets
whistling	working on cars	boating

List other skills or talents you have that aren't listed here.

_____

_____

Sometimes people think that if they feel depressed, they don't have any energy to help anyone else. What do you think about this?

_____

_____

_____

_____

Sometimes people think that since no one is helping them, they don't want to help anyone else. What is your opinion about this?

_____

_____

_____

_____

Choose one of the ideas from either of the lists above and describe what you think it would be like for you to try helping someone with this activity.

_____

_____

_____

_____

Tell whether or not you think that helping others might also help you, and why.

_____

_____

_____

_____

You can find people who need help in your life every day if you just look around. If you would like to try more organized volunteer work but don't know where to find it, start by calling your local hospital, place of worship, or village hall. You can also look on the Internet at www.networkforgood.org and www.volunteermatch.org.

you need to know

When people feel depressed, they may not have much energy. They may not have the desire to make plans because they don't have much interest in doing anything. Stopping activity, however, only increases depression. You can help yourself move past feelings of depression by staying actively involved in your life.

Eduardo's dad could tell that Eduardo was feeling depressed. He had parked himself in front of the television for four days in a row and channel-surfed for hours. When his friends called, Eduardo said he would call them back later, but he never did. When the family went out for pizza, Eduardo said he wasn't hungry. When his girlfriend came over to talk with him about going to a concert, Eduardo said he didn't feel like it.

Finally Eduardo's dad sat down to talk with him. He said he knew Eduardo didn't feel like doing anything, and he asked if not doing anything was helping Eduardo feel better. Eduardo said no; in fact, the less he did, the less he wanted to do. His dad explained that energy creates energy—you need to use energy to produce more of it. When Eduardo said he didn't even have any energy to start with, his dad challenged him to at least try. He suggested that Eduardo push himself to go to the concert and see how he felt when he got back.

It was all Eduardo could do to get up off the couch and change his clothes, but he did it. He thought it would be one of the hardest nights of his life and wondered how he would ever make it through. As he left home, he felt as if his body were made of lead, but his friends were excited and they put the band's CD on in the car. He liked the music a lot, and it seemed to pick him up a little. He guessed the concert might be fun, if he could stay awake.

When Eduardo got home that night, his dad was waiting up to see how it went. Eduardo said he never would have thought it possible, but he had left the house almost asleep and had come home full of energy. During the course of the night, he had forgotten his feelings of depression and found himself having a great time. He was amazed that his dad had been right.

directions

Under each of these five burners, write an activity you love to do that really energizes you. Above each burner, draw a flame that indicates how much energy you have when you are participating in this activity. If you have very little energy, draw a very low flame; if you have a great deal of energy, draw a very high flame.

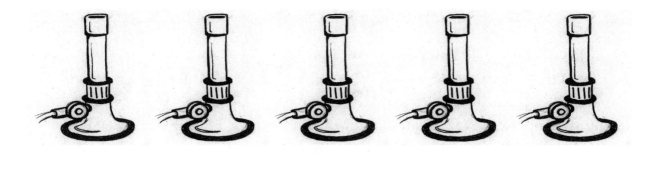

_____   _____   _____   _____   _____

Draw a flame above this burner that indicates how much energy you have when you are depressed.

more to do

Look back at the flames you drew and describe the difference between the amount of energy you have when you feel depressed and the amount of energy you have when you are doing something you love to do.

_____

_____

_____

Tell what you usually do when you are feeling depressed and don't have the desire or energy to do anything.

_____

_____

_____

Tell why you think that doing something you love could raise your energy level.

_____

_____

_____

Tell why you think it might be hard to push yourself to become active when you are feeling depressed.

_____

_____

_____

When you have little energy, it is sometimes easier to take a first step by doing small, simple activities. For example, it might seem more possible to e-mail or call a friend than to go to a party. In the list of activities below, put a number "1" next to those that seem like first steps for you and a number "2" next to those that seem like second steps.

____ play basketball	____ go to a movie
____ go to a concert	____ play cards
____ e-mail a friend	____ go to a party
____ go out to eat	____ call a friend
____ go for a walk	____ watch a basketball game
____ go to the pool or beach	____ play laser tag
____ play a video game	____ go to the mall
____ go to the library	____ go skateboarding
____ have a party	____ talk to a close relative
____ go to an amusement park	____ have one friend over

Make a list of any other first steps that could work for you.

_____

_____

Make a list of any other activities that raise your energy level.

_____

_____

_____

Make a commitment to yourself to try to stay active the next time you feel depressed, even if you don't feel like it at first.

food to help your mood

you need to know

Some research studies show that what people eat can affect their moods. Deficiencies in certain vitamins and nutrients have been linked to higher levels of depression. Paying attention to your diet and practicing healthy nutrition may help you prevent and relieve feelings of depression.

When the chemicals in our brains that regulate mood become imbalanced, depression can be triggered or escalate. Because the food that we put into our bodies affects the chemicals in our brains, eating particular foods can alter our moods.

While each person's chemical make-up is a little different, there are some vitamins and nutrients that have been shown to have an effect on brain chemicals in many people. These include the B-complex vitamins and folic acid in particular, omega-3 fatty acids, sugar, caffeine, and alcohol.

Vitamin B-12 is found in meat, dairy products, and eggs. All of the other B vitamins are found mainly in whole-grain products and fortified cereals, meats, leafy green vegetables, nuts, and seeds. Folic acid (vitamin B-9) is also found in citrus fruits, strawberries and cantaloupe, asparagus, liver, beans, and legumes (dried beans and peas). When your body is low in folic acid and other B vitamins, you may have more feelings of depression.

Omega-3 fatty acids are found in cold-water fish, such as tuna and salmon. These fatty acids have been found to play a crucial role in the function of brain chemicals. If your body is low in these acids, you may have stronger feelings of depression.

White sugar is found in candy, cookies, cakes, ice cream, soda, and many cereals. Caffeine is found in cola drinks, other sodas, tea, and coffee. Both of these substances have been linked to higher levels of depression. While sugar and caffeine may give an initial energy boost, the body's blood sugar then drops very quickly, and slowness and tiredness set in.

Alcohol is often used as an escape from depression, but since it affects the body by depressing the central nervous system, it actually makes depression worse. Alcohol also leads to vitamin deficiencies that can contribute to higher levels of depression.

Along with the information about particular foods that affect our brain chemicals, it is also important to know that a healthy diet is, in general, better for avoiding depression than one that is unhealthy. A healthy diet has a balance of fruits and vegetables, grains, proteins, and dairy products. It also includes a variety of foods from each of those categories. A healthy diet includes more fresh, natural foods and fewer processed or packaged foods. When you are eating a healthy diet, your body and mind function better and you are better able to handle the ups and downs of daily life. When you are eating an unhealthy diet, you have less physical and emotional energy to ward off feelings of depression.

directions

On the chart below, keep track of your food and beverage intake and your level of depressive feelings for one week. Record everything you eat or drink, and record your depression level three times each day. Rate your depression from 1 to 5, with 1 being very low and 5 being very high.

Day of the Week	Food and Beverage Intake	Depression Level (1-5)		
		One Hour After Waking	Midday	Evening
Monday				
Tuesday				
Wednesday				
Thursday				
Friday				
Saturday				
Sunday				

more to do

Look back at the information you have recorded about yourself. Do you see any patterns in your depression level? For example, do you seem to feel more depressed in the morning, afternoon, or evening?

_____

_____

_____

Compare the amount you eat of foods that may increase depression (sugar, caffeine, alcohol) to the amount you eat of foods that may decrease depression (those with B vitamins or omega-3 fatty acids). Describe what you notice.

_____

_____

_____

As you review your food consumption, determine if your diet is more healthy or unhealthy. Describe how you do or do not eat a balance of foods from different groups.

_____

_____

_____

Describe how you do or do not eat a variety of foods.

_____

_____

_____

Describe how you do or do not eat fresh and unprocessed foods.

_____

_____

_____

Describe any connection you notice between what you put into your body and your level of depression.

_____

_____

_____

Tell how you could realistically improve your diet to improve your mood.

_____

_____

_____

28 exercise and depression

you need to know

Physical exercise has the ability to improve mood and reduce feelings of depression. When people exercise, there is an increase in the production of the brain chemicals that lift their moods. Incorporating mild-to-moderate exercise into your daily life can help you feel less depressed.

When certain chemicals are released in our bodies, our moods rise and we gain a sense of well-being and happiness. When we exert our bodies through exercise, we both burn off stress chemicals and stimulate the production of the "happiness chemicals," helping to relieve symptoms of depression.

Exercise helps us feel better in other ways as well. When you exercise regularly, you can improve the condition of your muscles, become more coordinated, and improve your balance. These physical improvements transfer to emotional improvements; you gain emotional strength and mental coordination, and you have fewer mood swings.

When you exercise, you also increase your mastery over your body and mind. This empowerment helps give you the motivation and strength to let go of sadness and move ahead and to realize that you are not a victim and can make positive changes and improvements in your life.

Physically, exercise releases built-up emotion, helps you sleep better, improves your circulation, strengthens your heart, lowers your blood pressure, and improves your overall health. When you are physically healthy, you have more brainpower and energy to take on the challenges in your life. You feel less defeated and are less easily overwhelmed. The oxygen flow to your brain is increased, which helps you think clearly and rationally, increasing your ability to focus on the positive.

directions

Create an exercise plan for yourself for the next week. Start by deciding what type of exercise you enjoy. Circle any of the following that sound like fun to you:

biking	swimming	football	basketball
running	walking	yoga	tennis
dancing	skateboarding	surfing	Pilates
weight training	kick boxing	skiing	belly dancing
karate	baseball	hiking	volleyball

Add any other exercise you enjoy that isn't listed here. _____

_____

Now choose the activities you would like to do and set a realistic goal for yourself for this week. Over the next seven days, can you realistically do this activity once? Twice? Three times?

_____

Which days and which time of day can you fit this activity in?

_____

How much time will you have? Fifteen minutes? Twenty minutes? A half-hour?

_____

Realistic goals are those that you can easily accomplish. Do not plan to go skiing if you don't have the equipment, transportation, or money. Do not plan to play volleyball if there is no one who will play with you. Do not plan to start a running program if you really don't like running. Set a goal that you know you can achieve.

Record your realistic plan in the calendar below.

Day and Time	Planned Exercise

Pay attention to your levels of depression before and after exercising and record them as you go through the week.

Day	Depression Level Before Exercise					Depression Level After Exercise				
	1 Very Low	2	3	4	5 Very High	1 Very Low	2	3	4	5 Very High
	1 Very Low	2	3	4	5 Very High	1 Very Low	2	3	4	5 Very High
	1 Very Low	2	3	4	5 Very High	1 Very Low	2	3	4	5 Very High
	1 Very Low	2	3	4	5 Very High	1 Very Low	2	3	4	5 Very High
	1 Very Low	2	3	4	5 Very High	1 Very Low	2	3	4	5 Very High
	1 Very Low	2	3	4	5 Very High	1 Very Low	2	3	4	5 Very High
	1 Very Low	2	3	4	5 Very High	1 Very Low	2	3	4	5 Very High

more to do

Explain why you were or were not able to accomplish your exercise goals for the week.

_____

_____

If you didn't accomplish your goals, rewrite them here, making them more realistic. Think about what you need to change: the activity you chose, the amount of time you planned to spend, the days or times you had planned to exercise, and so on. Be as specific as possible. Then in the coming week, try again with your revised goals.

_____

_____

Look back at your rating scales and describe how your depression level was or was not affected by exercise.

_____

_____

Sometimes people find it hard to get motivated to exercise. You may find it helpful to do one of the following:

1. Get exercise-friendly clothing—shoes, shorts, leotard, or whatever you need for your activity. Having comfortable, appropriate clothes that you like can help you get psyched and enjoy your exercise more.

2. Try exercising to your favorite music. Upbeat music can lift your mood and energize you.

3. If you are more motivated in a social setting, try exercising with a friend or taking a class. Sometimes other people's energy helps boost yours, and the time can be social as well as physical.

4. If you're happier by yourself, don't force yourself into a group. Choose an activity you can do easily by yourself, such as running or walking. Always take safety precautions when you exercise alone.

breathwork 29

you need to know

Bringing an adequate supply of oxygen into the body helps people function better physically, emotionally, and mentally. When we are feeling depressed, we tend to take shallow breaths and sometimes even hold our breath for short periods without realizing it. Practicing healthy breathing techniques can help you release the physical and emotional feelings of depression and choose thoughts that will help you reduce depression.

When Lauren felt depressed, she noticed it all over. Her stomach felt queasy, and sometimes she experienced pressure on her chest. Her eyelids seemed to weigh a ton, and she had to drag herself from class to class at school. Her mood was low, she had a negative attitude, and her body didn't seem to want to move at all. One day when she was feeling especially depressed, Lauren went to see the school nurse. She just wanted to lie down on her couch for a while and take a nap. But after questioning Lauren about what was wrong, the nurse had another idea.

She explained that Lauren could help energize her body and release her feelings and thoughts of depression by taking more oxygen into her body. She taught Lauren a simple breathing exercise:

1. Sit quietly and comfortably.

2. Take as deep a breath as you can through your nose.

3. Hold the breath for a second or two.

4. Let the breath out as slowly as you can through your mouth.

5. Repeat the first four steps three times.

6. If you don't feel better, wait a few minutes and then do it again.

7. Repeat until you feel better.

At first, Lauren didn't think that breathing could help her at all. After all, she breathed every day, all day long, and she still got depressed. But after trying the exercise a few times with the nurse, she found that she did feel better. The discomfort in her stomach went away, and she didn't feel as tired. She was able to finish the day at school feeling fine and even made the decision to go out and have fun that night with her friends. Lauren continued to use the exercise whenever she noticed depressive symptoms coming on. She found she could both keep them from coming on so strongly and get them to go away faster.

directions

Find a place where you can try the breathing exercise that the nurse taught Lauren. Follow the directions above. Describe what it was like for you to do this exercise.

_____

_____

_____

The next time you feel depressed, pay attention to your breathing. Notice how far you take your breath into your body. Does it move all the way down into your lungs or your diaphragm? Or does it move in only as far as your nostrils or your throat? Record your observations here.

_____

_____

_____

Stop what you are doing and try the breathing exercise. Describe how it did or did not help you feel better.

_____

_____

_____

more to do

Most people are not used to paying attention to their breath, so it may seem unusual or feel uncomfortable to do an exercise like this at first. With practice, however, it will become easier, more familiar, and more comfortable.

Try another breathing exercise:

1. Sit quietly and comfortably.

2. Close your eyes.

3. "Find" your breath. Notice where it goes as it moves in and out of your body.

4. For the next few minutes, just pay attention to your breath. Notice where it goes within you. Notice how it feels or sounds as it moves in and out of your body. Don't consciously try to change your breathing in any way; just pay attention to it.

5. Continue to follow your breath until you feel peaceful.

Describe what it was like for you to do this breathing exercise. Was it more or less comfortable than the first one?

_____

_____

_____

Describe any change you noticed in your breath from the time you started the exercise to the time that you finished.

_____

_____

_____

Describe any change you felt in your body or your mood as you did this exercise.

_____

_____

_____

Tell why you do or do not think that a breathing exercise might help you relieve feelings of depression.

_____

_____

_____

creative expression 30

you need to know

Feelings that are not expressed can build up and damage people's physical and emotional health. One way to release feelings is through creative expression. Writing, art, movement, and music are all healthy ways to release feelings of depression.

Brett had been talking to a counselor outside of school for several months, trying to learn how to handle his feelings of depression. The counselor noticed that Brett had a hard time talking about his feelings, and other than her, there was no one he felt comfortable sharing them with. She also knew that Brett played drums in the school band. One day she suggested that Brett visit the Barn, an old house on the outskirts of town that had been converted into a coffee house. It was a place where local teens could hang out and also where they could experiment with different artistic mediums.

When Brett went to the Barn, he found lots of kids his own age participating in all kinds of artistic activities. A band was playing at one end of the large room, two girls were practicing ballet at a bar against the wall, several boys were working on a video production at the computer station, and there were tables and easels set up for art projects that were in the works. He also noticed a few kids sitting on couches and chairs in the corner, some drinking soda or juice, and some writing in notebooks.

On his first day there, Brett just wandered around exploring. The next time he visited, he hung around near the band. When they learned that he played drums, they asked if he wanted to jam with them for a while. Brett found it was more relaxing and creative than the structured music program at school. He found himself playing better than he ever had before, and he noticed that it made him feel good inside.

Brett started coming back regularly after that, usually playing drums with the band and sometimes bringing his notebook to share some of the science fiction stories he was working on. He met other kids who liked to write, and they shared ideas. At his counselor's suggestion, Brett tried expressing his feelings more, both in his music and his writing. At first he wasn't sure how to do that, but as he became more comfortable, he noticed he was working more from his heart than his head. He ended up both feeling better and discovering more creativity within himself. After a few weeks, Brett noticed that his feelings of depression had greatly diminished. He had found a safe and effective way to let them out.

directions

The nice thing about creative expression is that there is no wrong way to do it. You do not have to be able to play a particular song, write with certain words, create a particular type of picture, or move in one specific way. Creativity involves thinking in new ways or putting new variations on an old theme. It involves listening to your intuition and expressing feelings and thoughts that are uniquely you.

In the frame on the next page, practice creative expression by writing poetry or prose, drawing with color or without, or creating a collage that represents something you feel strongly about. Give your creation a title. Remember, there is no wrong way to complete this task.

more to do

On the scale below, mark how comfortable you feel about expressing yourself creatively.

1   2   3   4   5   6   7   8   9   10

Very Uncomfortable   Very Comfortable

Circle the method with which you feel most comfortable expressing yourself.

writing poetry	playing an instrument	dance
singing	writing stories	painting
drawing	photography	drama
sculpture	videography	recording arts
other _____		

Describe the places or situations where you feel most comfortable expressing yourself creatively.

_____

_____

Tell why you would or would not like to visit a place like the Barn.

_____

_____

Plan a time in the next few days when you can express yourself creatively. Afterward, describe what this was like for you. Tell how your feelings of depression were or were not affected by this activity.

_____

_____

you need to know

People who isolate themselves from others usually have a harder time dealing with depression than people who stay connected to supportive friends and family. Supportive people can act as a safety net to help hold us up emotionally during the harder times of life. Staying connected to people who encourage and support you will help you to manage feelings of depression.

When Amelia felt depressed, all she wanted to do was be alone. When her friends approached her at school, she didn't feel like talking, so she would try to avoid them. When her family ate dinner together, she ate quickly so that she wouldn't have to join in the conversation. Amelia felt like she would have to pretend to be happy if she was with other people, and it seemed so much easier just to keep to herself.

Amelia's older sister, Kate, noticed that Amelia was spending a lot of time in her room alone. When Kate asked what was wrong, Amelia said she didn't want to talk about it. But Kate told Amelia that she cared about her and didn't like to see her so sad. Finally Amelia told Kate how depressed she felt. Kate gave Amelia a big hug. She said she'd get them each a soda and then sit with Kate while they listened to their favorite CD together. It felt nice to Amelia that Kate was being understanding and trying to help. As they listened to the music, singing along with parts, she realized she felt a little better. After checking with their mom, Kate invited one of Amelia's best friends and one of her best friends to spend the night. The four girls sat up talking and watching movies, and Amelia found that everyone was kind and helpful when she shared her feelings with them. It made her feel good to be cared about and also to stop dwelling on her depressed feelings all by herself. She realized that staying connected to the supportive people in her life helped relieve her depression better than isolating herself.

directions

Draw a picture of yourself in the single frame below. In each of the frames that make up the safety net, draw a picture or write the name of someone in your life who could support or encourage you when you feel depressed. Think about all of your friends, family members, neighbors, teachers, coaches, and so on.

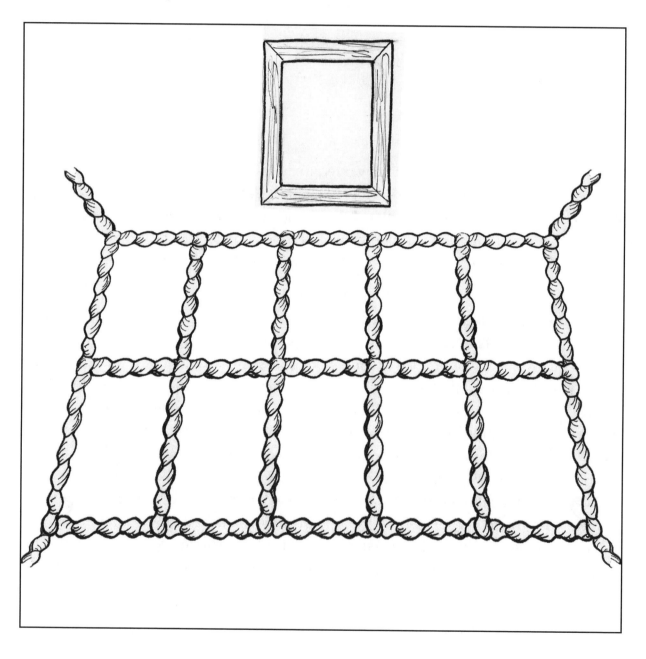

more to do

Tell why you may not want to talk to or be with anyone when you feel depressed.

_____

_____

_____

List each person you included in your safety net. Then describe how they encourage or support you. Do they listen, make you laugh, hug you, get you out of the house, give advice, or something else?

_____

_____

_____

Write the phone numbers and e-mail addresses of all of your support people below. Copy this information onto another piece of paper and keep it in your wallet, locker, or bedroom, or enter it into your cell phone so you can always get in touch with someone if you need to.

_____

_____

_____

Do you ever support or encourage anyone else when they need it? Describe what you do and whom you do it for.

_____

_____

_____

Someone once said, "Friendship divides our sorrows and multiplies our joys." When we share our sorrows with supportive people, it makes our problems feel smaller. When we share our good times, it makes our joy feel even bigger.

32 professional counseling

you need to know

One of the greatest helping tools for people with depression is talking to a counselor. Professional counselors are trained to help people understand why they feel depressed and find healthy ways to help themselves feel better. Professional counselors can provide emotional support and also teach coping skills so that you can learn to handle feelings of depression on your own.

When Zack's mom suggested he talk to a counselor about his depression, he told her, "No way." He said he didn't need any "shrink" to analyze his brain and tell him he was "psycho." Zack's mom asked if he thought his Uncle Brad was "psycho." Once again Zack said, "No way." Uncle Brad was a successful lawyer, had been the quarterback on his college football team, had a great sense of humor, and was an awesome chess player. Uncle Brad was one of Zack's favorite people.

Zack's mom told him to ask Uncle Brad what he thought about counseling, and the next time Zack saw him, he did. It turned out that Uncle Brad had a professional counselor that he had talked to when his mother died, when he and his wife were separated for a while, and when he was having trouble getting along with his son, Cody. Uncle Brad said that the counselor helped him to sort out things he was confused about and to identify the strengths within himself that would help him get through the hard times. The counselor also helped Uncle Brad and Cody learn how to get along better.

Zack was pretty amazed. He had thought counseling was only for people who were "crazy." But Uncle Brad was one of the coolest, most normal people Zack had ever met. When Zack told his mom he might reconsider talking to a counselor, she made him an appointment for the next week. John was a social worker who told Zack that he used to suffer from depression himself. He was easy to talk to and he helped Zack learn ways to manage and get over his feelings of depression. Zack felt a lot more positive and confident in himself after talking with John a few times. He decided counseling wasn't such a crazy thing after all.

directions

People can go to counselors for all different reasons, many of which are listed below.

Feeling nervous

Having a hard time getting along with your parents

Feeling bad about yourself

Feeling very sad because someone has died

Not getting along with people

Feeling afraid

Wanting to break a bad habit

Feeling sad

Having a hard time keeping up in school

Getting into fights

Parents getting divorced

Facing an illness

Feeling overwhelmed

Having a hard time concentrating

Feeling like running away

Getting into trouble

Wanting to hurt yourself

Not eating enough or eating too much

Abusing alcohol or drugs

Feeling lonely

Getting arrested

Other problems you have had

_____

Circle any of these problems that you may have had.

If you were to have an appointment with a counselor today, tell what you might want to talk about.

_____

_____

_____

_____

more to do

Describe what it feels like for you to think about talking to a counselor.

_____

_____

_____

Some people have the mistaken idea that it is a sign of weakness to go to a counselor. Actually, it takes strength to be able to face problems, and that's what you do in counseling. Tell your opinion about this.

_____

_____

Some people prefer a male counselor, and some prefer a female. Tell which you would prefer, and why.

_____

_____

Some people prefer to go to a counselor in their school, and some prefer to go to a counselor outside of their school. Tell which you would prefer, and why.

_____

_____

Most schools have a social worker, psychologist, or other counseling professional on their staff to help students with many types of problems, including dealing with feelings of depression. Make an appointment to meet with the professional counselor in your school—or any other professional counselor you may know—and ask them the following questions. Record their answers here.

What is your specific title? _____

What exactly do you do to help people? _____

_____

What kind of education did you have to get in order to do this job? _____

_____

Why did you want to be a counselor? _____

_____

Did you ever go to a counselor yourself? _____

_____

What kinds of problems do you help people with? _____

_____

How can counseling help someone with depression? _____

_____

Think of anything else you might want to ask a counselor before you share personal information with them. Write those questions here.

_____

_____

_____

Tell why you think a professional counselor could be helpful to you in managing feelings of depression.

_____

_____

_____

If you would like to talk to a counselor, tell your parent or another adult who can help you make an appointment.

33 group support

you need to know

People who feel depressed are often helped by sharing their feelings and experiences with others who are going through the same thing. Support groups bring people together to help each other by offering support and education about a problem. Sometimes support groups are run by professional leaders, and sometimes they are run by the members themselves. Getting involved in a support group can help you to better manage feelings of depression.

One day Kristen left the school cafeteria feeling very upset. She had just spent another lunch period pretending she was feeling great, when she was actually battling feelings of depression. She liked her friends and knew that they cared about her, but she couldn't talk to them about depression; none of them would understand. When she got to her locker, her friend Amy caught up with her and asked what was wrong. Kristen finally admitted that she felt very alone with her feelings and didn't have anyone to talk to. Amy shared with Kristen that she had been going to a weekly support group for girls with eating problems. The school nurse had started the group, which met after school on Mondays in her office. Amy said it really helped her to be with other girls who understood what she was going through, and also to get ideas for how to make things better. She suggested that a support group for kids who feel depressed might help Kristen.

Kristen thought about the idea and went to talk to the school nurse. The nurse said there was a group for teens with depression that met at the local Y. She gave Kristen the information, and Kristen went to her first meeting that week. At first she was nervous and almost changed her mind about going, but Amy encouraged her to give it at least one try. Once the group meeting started and Kristen began listening to the other kids talk about their feelings, her nervousness left. She felt so relieved to be with other people who felt like she did. The other kids were friendly and caring and fun to be with, and Kristen felt like she had found a second family. She continued going to the weekly meetings and found that she struggled with depression less and less as time went on.

directions

Quotes such as "Two heads are better than one" and "One hand washes the other" remind us that as humans we are all connected and function much better when we work together. Look at the business pages of a phone directory. In the space below, record as many services as you can that illustrate how people work together to help one another. For example, mechanics use their skills to help us with our cars, grocers provide us access to food, and so on.

By sharing information, goods, and services, we help each other meet our needs for daily living. Describe what needs you think a support group might help people meet.

more to do

Sometimes people are hesitant to join a group because they think they might not be comfortable with people they don't know. Describe any feelings like this that you may have now or have had in the past.

_____

_____

_____

If you are not comfortable talking with people you don't know well, read Activity 16: "Talking Tips from AL." Describe how you could apply the information in that activity to the idea of joining a support group.

_____

_____

_____

Talking about your personal feelings with other people might not feel comfortable at first. Tell what you think the difference might be between talking with people who don't know anything about depression and talking with people who have feelings of depression themselves.

_____

_____

_____

Tell what you hope would happen to help you if you joined a support group.

_____

_____

_____

_____

working as a family 34

you need to know

Events that happen in families and relationships between family members can contribute to feelings of depression. When people work as families to solve problems, depression can be relieved. Working together with your family members can help you understand the source of your depression and take steps to change it. Sometimes families can work things out on their own, and sometimes they need help from a counselor.

Every day, Sam felt more depressed. Ever since his grandpa died last summer, it seemed like his mom was yelling at his younger brother and him all the time. She was also working a lot of overtime, leaving his dad responsible for dinner, which meant they went out for fast food. The house seemed empty and sad.

Thomas's parents were getting divorced. When Thomas found out, he was angry and scared, but he didn't know what to do with his feelings. He didn't like going home from school anymore, and he was too embarrassed to tell his friends, so he started hanging out with a different group of kids. He knew they smoked pot, but he felt too depressed to care, so he went along with them.

Claire's dad traveled a lot for his job and was home only on weekends. Her mom was lonely and spent most of her evenings drinking martinis in front of the TV. Claire's brother completely ignored her; he tried to stay out of the house as much as possible so he wouldn't have to talk to their parents. When her boyfriend broke up with her, it seemed like the only person Claire could count on had left her. She felt so depressed that she wanted to run away.

All of these families needed to work together to solve their problems. Here's what happened:

One night, Sam approached his mom and told her that he missed her. He wanted her to stop working so late. He wanted things to be the way they used to be.

Sam's mom called his dad and brother into the room and asked if they felt the same way. They all did. They talked about how different things had been since Grandpa died. Sam's mom said she was very sad about losing Grandpa, and she realized now that she was working more so she didn't have to think about her sadness. But she didn't want to hurt her family. Sam's dad suggested that they make a scrapbook with all of their pictures of Grandpa, his favorite jokes and sayings, and the ribbons he had won at the state fair. They worked on the book together, and Sam's mom started coming home from work on time again and cooking dinner for them. Sam started feeling happy again instead of depressed.

Thomas was hanging out with his new friends in the field behind the school when a police car came by. Thomas was arrested for possession of marijuana, and the judge told his parents they must go to family counseling. During the counseling sessions, Thomas was able to tell his parents how angry he was about their divorce. He also told them about his fears of never seeing his dad again once he moved out. With the counselor's help, his mom and dad listened to his feelings and reassured Thomas that they understood his anger. Then they worked out a plan for Thomas to see his father every weekend and on all school holidays. Thomas's feelings of depression lifted, and he started caring about himself again.

One night when Claire and her brother came home, they found their mother passed out on the couch and they couldn't wake her up. They called 911, and an ambulance took her to the hospital. They called their father, who flew home that night. The social worker at the hospital told Claire and her brother that her mother needed treatment for alcohol addiction. As part of that treatment, the family would be asked to come to counseling sessions at the hospital. During those sessions, the four of them talked about the good things in their family and also the things that were not so good. They talked about what they would like to be different in their family. Claire's father talked to his boss about changing his job responsibilities so he could travel less. Claire's mother agreed to stop drinking. These changes made Claire's brother enjoy his parents more, and he began spending more time with the family. Claire was able to get more support and caring from her parents, and she didn't feel as depressed anymore.

directions

Draw a picture of your family members in a circle in the center box below. Space them evenly. Draw smooth lines between the members who get along well and jagged lines between the members who do not get along well. Draw partially smooth and partially jagged lines between the members who get along well at some times and poorly at others.

In the frame around the center box, write or draw events and circumstances that affect your family. These may be positive or negative and could include divorce, job issues, legal issues, financial issues, health issues, or relationships with others outside of your family.

When you are done, circle the family members, relationships, or outside issues that have an effect on your level of depression. Then put a star by those that affect you the most.

more to do

Tell what your first impression is when you look at what you have drawn. How does it make you feel?

_____

_____

Describe how and why the items you starred affect your feelings of depression.

_____

_____

_____

Describe what you would like to see change in your family to help you feel less depressed.

_____

_____

Tell which of these things are possible and which may not be possible.

_____

_____

Tell whether or not you think your family could work these things out by talking together.

_____

_____

Tell how you think a counselor might help your family make positive changes.

_____

_____

Share this activity with your parents or another member of your family. Talk about how you can work together to make positive changes in your family.

weighing the consequences 35

you need to know

People who feel so depressed that they think they want to hurt themselves can help to stay safe by thinking about the consequences of their actions. While they may feel so down that they wish they weren't alive, if they weren't, there would be many negative repercussions. Stopping to think about the consequences of hurting yourself can help you realize that it is not a good idea.

Maria was sitting alone outside the school behind the field house, thinking about how worthless her life was. She wondered if anyone would even notice if she weren't here anymore. Maybe if she were gone, people would wonder about her. Maybe then she would finally be noticed. Tears ran down her face as she thought about how depressed she felt.

A noise behind her startled her. It was her friend, Jeremy, who had lived next door to her since second grade. Jeremy was at her house so often that he was more like a brother than a friend. Jeremy saw Maria crying and asked what was wrong. Maria told him how useless she felt, how empty and insignificant she felt her life was.

Jeremy was surprised. Didn't she realize what would happen if she weren't here? What would he do without her? He counted on seeing her every day, even if just for a few minutes. He said there was no one else who knew him like she did, and accepted him. There was no one else he trusted as much as Maria. He would be lonely without her.

What about her family? If she were gone, her parents would be sad all the time. Her little sister would have to be alone after school instead of having Maria to watch her. What if she got hurt? How would it affect her if Maria hurt herself? And Maria's grandmother, who called Maria her "little flower," might lose her will to live if Maria were gone.

Even Ruby, Maria's cat, would miss sleeping on her feet at night. What if Ruby went looking for Maria and got lost or got hit by a car? And what about Mrs. Menzer? Maria watered her prize flowers every week all summer long because Mrs. Menzer was confined to the house. What would she do without Maria?

And what about all the future children Maria was going to help when she became a pediatrician? Maria might find a cure for some childhood disease and might save a lot of lives, but that would never happen if she didn't stay alive.

Jeremy was about to keep going, but Maria told him to stop. She said she hadn't thought about these consequences; she had only thought about how bad she felt. She said that she wouldn't want to hurt all those other people just to take away her own hurt. She said she guessed that maybe her life wasn't completely useless after all.

directions

Write your name in the blank spaces in the sentences below, and then ask two people who know you well to answer the following questions about you. You may ask the questions and record the answers or make a copy of this page and give it to them to write their own answers.

What is one of the best times you've ever had with _____?

_____

_____

What qualities do you value most about _____?

_____

_____

Why is _____ important in your life?

_____

_____

How would you feel if _____ were gone from your life?

_____

_____

How is the world a better place by having _____ in it?

_____

_____

Who else do you know who values _____'s presence in their life?

_____

_____

more to do

People who think their lives are insignificant may not realize that each person in the world, including themselves, plays an important role in the universe. Pretend that someone you care about doesn't see any reason to live anymore. Write that person a letter telling what the consequences would be if he or she were no longer alive.

_____

_____

_____

_____

_____

_____

_____

_____

_____

_____

_____

_____

If you have ever felt that no one would care if you lived or died, describe what you were thinking and feeling here.

_____

_____

_____

Write yourself a letter describing what the consequences would be if you were no longer alive. Write it as if you cared about yourself deeply.

_____

_____

_____

_____

_____

_____

_____

_____

_____

_____

_____

_____

_____

_____

_____

_____

_____

If you have feelings of not wanting to live, it is important that you share your feelings with a parent, teacher, counselor, or other responsible adult. Put this book away now, and find someone whom you can tell.

36 sharing your feelings

you need to know

Sometimes people's feelings of depression become very extreme and may appear to be unbearable. When depression feels this overwhelming, people may feel so tired and so sad that they wish they were not alive. Sometimes they don't stop to think clearly, and they try to hurt themselves or take their own life. If you ever have feelings that are this strong, it is very important to keep yourself safe by telling someone else how you feel.

Sadness almost always feels bigger when you keep it to yourself. If you are ever feeling so depressed that you think you want to hurt yourself, it is important that you share your feelings with someone else. This will help to diminish your feelings of depression, and it will also alert other people so that they can either help you or get help for you.

Sometimes when people are depressed, they feel very alone and they may think that no one cares about them. This is rarely true. The depressive feelings may just be so big that it is hard to see past them to the people who are there waiting to help.

All around you are people who can help you, but they cannot help you if they don't know how you feel. Sometimes people give clues to how they feel by acting destructively or aggressively. But clues aren't always enough. If you feel so depressed that you might hurt yourself, it is very important to tell someone directly.

directions

Next to the titles below, write the names of people in your life whom you could tell if you ever felt so depressed that you might try to hurt yourself.

Parent _____

Friend _____

Neighbor _____

Teacher _____

Coach _____

Relative _____

Doctor _____

Counselor _____

Worship leader _____

Other _____

Write the words you would use when you talk to this person. Tell what you are feeling and tell what you are afraid of. Tell if you are thinking of hurting yourself. There are no right or wrong ways to say it. Just be clear and speak from your heart.

_____

_____

_____

_____

_____

_____

_____

more to do

Describe your worst feelings of depression. Tell when they occurred and how long they lasted.

_____

_____

_____

Rate your current feelings of depression on the scale below according to whether or not you feel you might hurt yourself.

```
|---+---+---+---+---+---+---+---+---+---|
0   1   2   3   4   5   6   7   8   9   10
```

I can confidently
say that I do not
feel at all like
hurting myself.

I am very afraid I
might do something
to hurt myself.

If your rating was above zero (0), plan to share these feelings with someone as soon as you can. Tell whom you will share them with and when you will do it.

_____

_____

_____

_____

_____

If you are not sure how to put your feelings into words, you can share this workbook and show what you have written in this activity.

Sit quietly and close your eyes for a moment. Picture yourself sharing your feelings with the person you have chosen. Picture yourself asking that person to help keep you safe. Picture the feeling of relief and reassurance you feel when you tell.

After you have shared your feelings, describe what happened.

_____

_____

_____

_____

Fill your name in the first blank space. Then ask the person you have told to complete and sign the statement below.

You, _____, have told me that you are very depressed

and feel you might hurt yourself. I care about you and will not let

this happen. I will keep you safe by _____

_____.

Signed _____

If you have ever felt that you might hurt yourself, or if you do now, be sure to read and complete Activities 35 through 40 in this book. It will be best if you share what you write or do the activities with an adult.

37 an emergency plan

you need to know

When people feel very depressed, they cannot always think clearly. If you are not thinking clearly, you may not be able to take care of yourself the way that you need to. Creating an emergency plan while you are feeling good gives you an effective tool to keep yourself safe if you are ever not thinking clearly.

The social worker at Jenna's school was giving a talk on how to handle emergencies. She went over information about how to handle physical emergencies at home, at school, and in a car. She taught some basic first aid and she also talked about "emotional emergencies." She explained that when people are very upset emotionally, they may not be able to think clearly enough to act in safe ways. She said that people who are very depressed may do something to hurt themselves that they wouldn't have done if they were feeling better or thinking clearly. She explained that having an emergency plan for these situations could help keep people safe.

Jenna talked to the social worker the next day and said she'd like to create an emotional emergency plan for herself because she felt very depressed at times. The social worker told her to make a list of all the things that she knew helped her come out of depression and all the people who could help her if she felt very down. Then they looked over her lists together and made up the following plan:

Jenna's Emotional Emergency Plan

Step 1: Stop thinking about whatever is making me feel depressed—right now. Put my mind on something that makes me feel good.

Step 2: Take a few deep breaths so I can help myself think clearly.

Step 3: Make a list of all the good things in my life, including everything I can think of.

Step 4: Remind myself of all the times I have gotten through hard situations in the past.

Step 5: Remind myself that this feeling is only temporary, and it will pass.

Step 6: Talk to my mom, my best friend Lindsay, my aunt Sarah, or my counselor, and tell them how I feel.

Jenna made four copies of her plan. She put one in her locker, one in her purse, and one in her night-table drawer, and she gave one to her mom. Once her plan was in place, Jenna felt confident that she could get through a hard time with depression without doing anything that might hurt her.

directions

Following Jenna's example, make a list of all the things that you know would help you to come out of depression and all the people who could help you if you feel extremely depressed. Write your own emotional emergency plan below. Make as many copies as you need and put them in places where they will be handy if you need them.

_____

_____

_____

_____

_____

_____

_____

_____

_____

_____

_____

_____

_____

_____

_____

_____

more to do

Have you ever felt so depressed that you weren't able to think clearly? Describe what this was like and what happened.

_____

_____

_____

_____

_____

_____

Think about what you know about yourself and how events in your life affect you. Write down any situations where you think an emotional emergency plan could be helpful for you.

_____

_____

_____

_____

Share your answers to the previous question with someone you trust. Talk about how you will act if any of these situations ever arise. Then choose at least two other people to share your emergency plan with. Write their names here and tell why you chose them.

_____

_____

_____

Sit quietly for a moment and close your eyes. Picture yourself at a time when you feel very depressed. Picture yourself taking out your emergency plan at that moment and one by one, putting the steps you have chosen into action. Picture yourself finding help and relief by using your plan. Picture yourself feeling better.

38 signing a contract

you need to know

A contract is an official agreement or commitment between two parties or with yourself. When you sign a contract, you agree to honor that commitment under all circumstances. Signing a contract that states you will not hurt yourself is a commitment to keeping yourself safe even if you feel very depressed.

Matt was talking to his counselor, Elizabeth, about how depressed he felt. He said he was so down and hurting so badly that he had thought about ending his life. He just didn't have the energy to face his problems anymore.

Elizabeth asked him if he really would hurt himself or if it was just a fantasy but not something he would really do. Matt wasn't sure. He just knew that he felt very bad and he really didn't want to be here anymore.

Elizabeth said that Matt needed to make a commitment to staying safe and staying alive. She knew that things in his life would get better, that the depressive feelings would subside, and that Matt could withstand this difficult time, even if he didn't believe it right now. She asked if Matt could promise her that he would keep himself safe for the next twenty-four hours. Matt thought about it and said yes. He could make it through the next day. Elizabeth said she wanted his promise in writing. She asked Matt to write and sign a contract stating that he would not do anything to hurt himself in the next twenty-four hours. This is what he wrote:

I, Matt Harris, hereby promise that I will not do anything to harm myself in any way for twenty-four hours from when I write this contract.

If I do feel like hurting myself, I will call my dad, my mother, or my counselor and I will tell them how I feel and ask for help.

I give my word that I will keep this promise and not break this contract.

I am committed to keeping myself safe.

Matt signed and dated the contract, and Elizabeth signed it also. She made one copy for herself, one for Matt, and one for Matt's parents. She told Matt to choose activities during the next twenty-four hours that would be safe for him. She told him to be with other people rather than being alone. She told him that when twenty-four hours was up, they would write another contract. Matt agreed. He realized that having written and signed the contract made him feel better, and he was more confident that he could keep himself safe.

directions

If you feel that you are currently in danger of harming yourself in any way, it is important that you tell someone right away. Take the time right now to put this workbook down, find a responsible adult, and tell that person how you feel. Then share this activity and write a contract for yourself, making a commitment to keep yourself safe for twenty-four hours or longer.

IMPORTANT NOTE

If you cannot agree to make this commitment, you need to tell a responsible adult. If you are alone, you need to find or call a responsible adult and tell them how you feel. If you cannot reach anyone, call 911 or go to your nearest hospital emergency room.

If you are not currently in danger of hurting yourself, write a contract that states that if you ever do feel that way, you will take all necessary steps to keep yourself safe.

_____

_____

_____

_____

_____

_____

_____

_____

_____

more to do

In your own words, tell what making a commitment means.

_____

_____

_____

Has anyone ever made a promise or a commitment to you and then broken it? Describe what this was like and how you felt.

_____

_____

_____

People make a number of important commitments in their life. They might commit to helping a friend, being on a team, keeping a confidence, taking a job, getting married, and so on. Explain why it is important to honor the commitments you make.

_____

_____

_____

Explain why you will honor any commitment you make to keeping yourself safe.

_____

_____

_____

It is important to make a commitment to keep yourself safe every day of your life. Even if you feel very depressed and at the moment cannot remember that things will get better, you need to commit to not harming yourself in any way. Then you will make it through the most difficult time and you will be able to enjoy your life again when the feelings of depression are gone.

39 hotlines to help

you need to know

There are many places you can go and people who are ready to help you twenty-four hours a day, seven days a week, if you ever feel so deeply depressed that you are thinking of harming yourself in any way. No matter where you live, every community provides some kind of free services for people in this situation. Help is available to you at all times, whatever your age, race, religion, gender, or circumstances. Knowing about these specific resources in your community can help keep you safe.

The following are services designed to help you if you are afraid you may hurt yourself:

911: In most areas of the United States, dialing 911 on your telephone will connect you with an instant emergency service. The people who answer the phone are ready to get help to you within minutes of receiving your call.

Phone lines: When you call a telephone crisis line, you will have the chance to express your thoughts and feelings to someone who is trained to listen to you and help you. Phone counselors are trained to hear your story and your pain with an objective ear. They are also taught to get you the help that you need to stay safe. Often they can recommend a place that you can go for additional help or resources. Some people feel more comfortable sharing information with a phone counselor because this is not someone in their personal life. They have anonymity and they do not have to feel embarrassed by their situation.

Hospital emergency rooms: All hospitals are required by law to help people who have hurt themselves or are in danger of hurting themselves, no matter who they are and whether or not they have money to pay for services. If you are ever in need of help or feel that you might do harm to yourself, you can go to the nearest hospital emergency room, and people there will take care of you. If you do not know where the nearest hospital is, call information (411) on your phone. If you are traveling or are in a community far from your home, you still have the right to receive services.

directions

Use your local phone directory, ask an adult to help you, or call directory assistance (411) on your phone, and find all the information necessary to fill out the Hotlines to Help card below.

Hotlines to Help

911

Fire Department emergency number: _____

Police Department emergency number: _____

Hospital emergency rooms: _____

Crisis lines: _____

Crisis intervention services: _____

Make a copy of this card and place it near the phone in your house, or program the numbers into your cell phone. Keep a copy of it in your wallet or somewhere else so it will be available if you need it.

more to do

The fact that our society provides emergency services for its residents reflects the fact that we value each individual life, including yours. Sometimes you may not feel like anyone cares, but in reality, very many people do. Have you ever smiled at a stranger or opened a door for someone you don't know? Describe caring actions you have shown to other people.

_____

_____

_____

Every time you give to someone else, you contribute to the good that is in the world. And you deserve just as much to be cared about and given help yourself. People you don't even know are working to help keep you safe. They have taken these jobs because they want to help others. Tell which of the emergency services you would use first if you needed them.

_____

_____

_____

For some people, it is hard to reach out for help. But once they do, they usually feel relieved. Tell why you think this is.

_____

_____

_____

Your life is valuable, and there are people who want to help you. Find another person to show this exercise to. Make a promise to yourself and that person that if you ever need help from emergency services, you will reach out and ask for it. Write your promise here. Sign your name and date it.

_____

_____

_____

_____

_____

_____

_____

_____

_____

_____

_____

_____

40 the power of hope

you need to know

Even the worst feelings of depression get better, but sometimes people are so focused on the pain of the moment that they forget this fact. When this happens, it can make any situation appear hopeless, even if it is not. You can keep depressive feelings from becoming overwhelming by using the power of hope.

Carl had been struggling with feelings of depression for almost a year. Usually he could manage his feelings pretty well, but in the last week he felt like he was losing ground. His dad had been injured in a car accident and was in the hospital intensive care unit. Carl was very frightened that his dad might die. He had gone to visit his dad every day, but it made him so upset that he wasn't able to eat or sleep much. He had missed three days of school, including two big tests that he needed good grades on in order to pass the classes. Carl felt very tired, and his sadness felt so big that he didn't know how he could survive.

The day Carl was feeling the worst, he went to the hospital again. This time his grandmother was there. She was sitting next to his dad's bed, patting her son's hand. She had a loving smile on her face. Carl dropped into the other chair, exhausted and overwhelmed. His grandmother saw the deep sadness on his face and asked if he was okay. Carl said no, he was very depressed. His dad would die, and he would flunk out of school and be depressed forever. His grandma came over and put her arm around him. She felt surprisingly strong.

"Carl," she said, "you don't have to let your feelings of depression get the best of you. You are so focused on your pain that you've lost sight of hope. There is great hope that your dad will pull through this. He was in good physical health before the accident. His heart is strong and so is his will to live. He has shown a little improvement every day. There is also hope that your teachers will understand this extreme situation when you explain it to them. They may let you take your tests over again or do extra work to pick up your grades. There is hope that your feelings of depression are temporary, too. You have the strength to get through this, just as you have gotten through other challenges, and soon you will feel better."

Carl listened to his grandmother. What she said made sense. He just hadn't seen the hope because he had been too focused on the depression. He realized that he didn't have to feel as bad as he did—there was great hope that everything would turn out all right.

directions

Each of the kids in the situations below is feeling overwhelmed with depression. Write a statement of hope about their situation that could help them out of their deep sadness.

_____
_____
_____
_____
_____
_____
_____
_____

_____
_____
_____
_____
_____
_____
_____
_____

_____
_____
_____
_____
_____
_____
_____
_____

more to do

Tell why you think that people sometimes focus on depression instead of hope.

_____

_____

_____

_____

Explain what you think is meant by this statement of hope: "It's always darkest before the dawn."

_____

_____

_____

_____

Describe a situation in the past when you had lost sight of hope. Tell what eventually happened. Did the worst thing happen? Did you survive? Did things eventually get better?

_____

_____

_____

_____

Describe any situations in your life right now that are causing you to feel depressed. Write a realistic statement of hope about each one.

_____

_____

_____

_____

Lisa M. Schab, LCSW, is a licensed clinical social worker with a private counseling practice in the Chicago suburbs. She writes a monthly parenting column for *Chicago Parent* magazine and is the author of eight self-help books and workbooks for children and adults. Schab teaches self-help and relaxation therapy workshops for the general public and professional training courses for therapists. She received her bachelor's degree from Northwestern University and her master's degree in clinical social work from Loyola University.

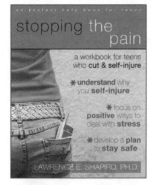